Every once in a while a book comes along
that has great impact on the world,
its societies, its belief systems, its people.
The impact of *Voyage To The New World*
will be measured in these terms.

VOYAGE TO THE NEW WORLD

RAMTHA

WITH

DOUGLAS JAMES MAHR

FIRST EDITION

MASTERWORKS, INC.

Publishers

Friday Harbor, Washington

MASTERWORKS, INC.
Publishers
Post Office Box 1847
Friday Harbor, Washington 98250

First Edition,
Third Printing; September 1986

Interior and cover design by
Rickabaugh Design,
Portland, Oregon

Typestyle set in Century Schoolbook by
King Typesetting and Printing,
Friday Harbor, Washington

Printed by R.R. Donnelley & Sons Company,
The Lakeside Press,
Crawfordsville, Indiana

The quotation on page six is from *The World Aloft* by Guy Murchie. Copyright© 1960 by Guy Murchie. Reprinted by permission from Houghton Mifflin Company.

Library of Congress Cataloging in Publication Data

Ramtha, the enlightened one.
  Voyage to the new world.

    Bibliography: p.
    1. Spirit writings.   2. Spiritualism.   I. Mahr,
    Douglas James, 1946-   .   II. Title.
BF1301.R235   1985   133.8   85-4865
ISBN 0-931317-33-9, Hardcover
ISBN 0-931317-34-7, Trade Paperback

▲

Reader, Please Note

This book, *Voyage To The New World*, is a compilation of a portion of the writings of J.Z. Knight and the writings of Douglas James Mahr. J.Z. Knight is the channel for the unseen entity, Ramtha, The Enlightened One. The writings of J.Z. Knight as expressed herein, are known at large as the truth of the entity Ramtha, The Enlightened One. Douglas James Mahr is one of Ramtha's named scribes. This compilation was researched, transcribed, edited, and proofed by Douglas James Mahr. Other members of *Masterworks, Inc., Publishers* assisted in transcribing, inputting to word processing equipment, and proofreading.

Some of Ramtha's words and/or phrases, particularly, "as it were indeed," "indeed," and "that which is termed," were deleted by scribe Mahr. You will also note that Ramtha occasionally speaks a sentence both in the present and the past tense, and has created a number of new words for contemporary dictionaries. You will also notice a few unusual usages. In all instances, words not known or used rarely in the twentieth century were searched for applicable meaning. Those words discovered while searching various sources were left intact. Some words not found were deleted. Some words without contemporary definition were left intact if their assumed meaning did not distract from possible contemporary interpretation. Bracketed words indicate co-author Mahr's deletions and/or additions.

Italicized words were selected by Mahr to add emphasis and clarity. Capitalization was also selected by Mahr to add depth of meaning to ordinary words which were used with extraordinary significance by Ramtha. Capitalization is not consistent due to the vast array of meanings imparted by Ramtha.

In summary, this work is an accurate representation of many varied and significant expressions by Ramtha, The Enlightened One, via the writings of J.Z. Knight, that have been compiled and developed into the *Voyage To The New World* theme by named scribe, Douglas James Mahr.

About *Douglas James Mahr*

Douglas James Mahr has traveled the world in search of adventure into the unknown worlds. Mahr's first meeting with Ramtha was in February, 1981. Mahr was amazed by what he heard and witnessed. Ramtha, an entity of apparently unlimited dimension channeled by J.Z. Knight, was presenting new information in our search for human fulfillment. Mahr saw Ramtha's communications as possibly the most deliberate attempt ever to be made by the unseen world to interact with planet Earth.

Mahr bought or borrowed any tape of those early conversations he could find, trying to ascertain the validity of the transmissions. For four years Mahr listened to tapes and observed J.Z. Knight and her constant, unseen companion, Ramtha. He interviewed many who had experienced Ramtha's realities. The conclusions of Mahr's research are presented herein for your consideration. The result is an exploration in self-discovery, a navigational aid to communication with our ultimate human potential.

Douglas James Mahr has been involved in the publication of nine books, including a book for children, *The Ominous Dragoon,* also co-authored with Ramtha.

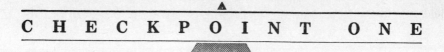
THE WILDEST OF DARING ADVENTURES

THE PURSUIT OF SELF

B O N   V O Y A G E

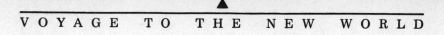

You are about to embark upon a voyage of exploration. This book is an expedition into an unseen world, a world of unlimited dimension explored by only a few. You are one of those pioneer explorers, comparable in stature to Columbus, to Lindbergh, and to those who showed us the passageway to the summit of Everest. Your courage matches the courage of those who rode the rockets to the moon. Your spirit matches the spirit of all of those who have shown us another world to see. You are the pioneers of a world grander and more vast than imagination.

I welcome you aboard this fantastic adventure. *Voyage To The New World* will open to you new worlds of unseen realities, realities just beyond your dreams. This book was created to transport you on a voyage into the world of the unseen. The words herein are a glimpse of what exists out there, out there beyond your eyes, beyond your mind, beyond your senses.

Why would you want to sail along with me on a voyage into an unseen world? Perhaps you are just plain curious about what a new world could be like, a new world filled with new realities. And quite possibly this new world could be the world of your dreams; after all, realities are what dreams are made of. Or maybe you want to sail along with me because you desire to answer some of your unanswered questions, questions about what you are and what your birthright is. And I bet you want to manifest many of your wants and desires; I bet you want to live in absolute abundance.

Perhaps the world, as you see it, seems a little bit out of control to you. Then I *know* you will want to sail into the tomorrows of your dreams, those dreams that cry to bring forth a new world of understanding and peace, freedom and joy. These are all lofty ideals and they are *all* within your reach. During this voyage you will delve into many areas currently off limits to thought. Your delving will birth the ideals of the new world, and your courage to delve will lead you into the tomorrows of your dreams.

This book could give birth to a new definition of heroism. What is it to be a pioneer hero to yourself? Unto what heights can you lead yourself to discovery? What new-world thoughts of yours will be harvested to become the actions of tomorrow? And how will *you* blossom into the tomorrows of your dreams?

Science Fiction Has Become Science Fact

Today we live in a world bursting at its seams, bursting to go beyond what it seems to be. The reality we see appears blurred; justice seems unjust, truth looks like untruth, things feel like they're out of our hands, with a destiny of their own. Acceptable answers are few and far between. Many of us have become, out of necessity, explorers and adventurers, seeking the heights to expand our sight beyond what we *think* we know. That quest is leading us beyond the seen world, a world that we find familiarity in, to a world known only as the unseen, a world filled with explanation and reason. There, many of us believe we can delve into the unlimitedness of thought, into the depths of forever, to derive answers for living today, in the moment.

Today boundaries are being stretched. Many are discovering the unlimitedness of their Self, discovering that *they* are the only limiters of their worlds. Many are pushing forward the boundaries into a new age; an age of complete knowingness, an age of complete and instantaneous manifestation of thought, an age of total life. We are on the verge of discovering the unseen worlds beyond. Those places that live in other dimensions are now our playgrounds of adventure. Science fiction is becoming science fact. We are at the crossroads.

This book was designed as a navigational aid to assist you through unfamiliar, murky waters into this unseen new world. Navigation, as it was first used in its infancy, was annotated in some of the earliest literature of humankind. According to biblical history, Noah, during the flood, sent forth a dove, ". . . but the dove found no rest for the sole of her foot and she returned unto him into the ark." A few days later Noah tried again. The dove returned that evening with an olive leaf in her beak. She allowed Noah to discover two very important facts; the waters had receded from the earth, and the direction from which the dove flew back to him, north by northeast. He simply charted his course north by northeast and soon Noah could shout, "Land ho!"

The exploratory tools of navigation lead the navigator to the discovery of precise facts. Those precise facts are then reasoned and applied to accepted knowledge available to ascertain direction and progress. With the use of various methods, the navigator ascertains where he has been, where he is now, and where he can expect to be in the future. Therefore, navigation has been defined as the pursuit of truth. In much the same way that a navigator leads his pilot to land, you will use navigation as you embark upon your voyage into the unseen world.

In the early days of navigation, methods were utilized which gave a "guess and by gosh" method of navigation. In some instances they worked, in others they missed their mark. Probably the best known incident of missing the mark was when Columbus bumped into an unknown land that simply wasn't supposed to be there, it existed on no known charts. The unseen world of Columbus' discovery was, of course, the North American continent. Were you a mariner actually aboard ship with Columbus, you could have observed his navigational methods. wind bearings that blew his sailing vessels along certain known trade-wind routes; dead reckoning; simple visual indication of north from the North Star; compass directional viewpoints; vague judgments of latitude by guessing the attitude of the pole; fathom soundings; and a lot of guessing and by-goshing.

Ninety-eight percent of the navigator's art in 1492 was dead reckoning. Dead reckoning today is still important to navigation. However, because of the technical advances of instrumentation, D.R. (as it is abbreviated) is only utilized during clear and unlimited weather conditions. Yet, in the case of instrument failure, dead reckoning has saved many a life. Dead reckoning was originally called deduced reckoning. It was shortened to *ded. reckoning* and then punned to *dead reckoning.* According to Guy Murchie in his book, *The World Aloft,* "It is simply the process of keeping track of how fast you are going, in what direction, and when you change to other speeds or directions. It means plotting your hourly and daily positions on your chart as you go, and being able to deduce the net result of your various trackings into a definite position for any moment of time."

The technological age has brought forth quantum-leap advances in navigation. Navigation via instruments now allows the pilot to see through to the contours of unseen lands. Yet, even today, no known instruments in this country exist to show us what could be out there in an unseen world, the world just beyond our limited realities. However, presently, we do have two reliable navigational methods available to us to assist us in the exploration of the unseen world. We can use deduced reasoning; that will allow us to know where we've been, where we are, and where we're heading along our journey of discovery. And we can utilize a unique navigational aid just now emerging in the 1980's—communication with the unseen world via thought and speech.

This book then, provided as a navigational aid, is the product of three entities—one lives in the unseen world and two live in this, the seen world: J.Z. Knight is a woman who channels a personality who calls himself Ramtha, The Enlightened One; Ramtha is a unique entity who exists in the unseen world while interacting with the seen world; and Douglas James Mahr is an author who has observed J.Z. Knight's and Ramtha's interaction with thousands of people since 1981. All three have been a part of this grand adventure, this voyage into the unseen, as are you.

The Adventures Of Your Tomorrows Here Today

Wild, daring adventures are thought to be those that break records, make millions, gain fame, establish world-at-your-feet respect and prestige, and ultimately lead to the un-bridled ability to wield power. Yet, your adventures of tomorrow will be the wildest of wild adventures—those adventures will lead you to the unlimitedness of your universes and will live in forever. This voyage into the un-seen world is an exploration of your total unlimitedness. You, as the fearless explorer, will soon realize that *you* are the maker of your destinies.

The unseen world, as many know it today, is a world of enigma, mystery, danger and fear. It is a world that many of us know is there yet we try to ignore it most of the time. We hear about our friends who talk to unseen entities, and we read about unseen personalities writing books telling us about the great unknown. Some of it makes sense, sounds good, gives us something to do on a Saturday night. Yet, we are skeptical and for good reason. Unseen personalities have been classified in a world of hocus-pocus rather than the world of friend and teacher. In the motion picture and television world they have been portrayed as things to avoid. How many of us in our childhood have been scared under the covers after seeing a Saturday horror matinee? Remember those terrifying scenes that depicted a wild, un-seen horribleness living out there in the darkness that was just waiting to devour you?

These horrific depictions of the unseen world are quite outmoded now. *Close Encounters of a Third Kind*, a major movie of the 1970's, portrayed entities from beyond our planet as loving, compassionate beings intent on the nurturing of our human friendship rather than our destruction. Conversely, it was only a few decades ago when we were chilled with H.G. Wells' *War of the Worlds*, which depicted space creatures intent upon our destruction. If the thinking of the times can be gauged by the popularity of a movie, then it would appear that in the 1950's it was popular to believe that space invaders were planning to destroy us. And conversely, in the 1980's, a space invader is just someone who beats you to your special table at your favorite restaurant.

What this change of attitude has brought forth is a whole new acceptance of the possibility of the existence of a world beyond what we see, a world that could be in the unseen. And even more revolutionary is the notion that that new world could help us along our paths to the discovery of the abundance of life. This new attitude is becoming known as an attitude of unlimitedness — an attitude of individual knowingness that also allows everyone else their *own* truth.

New On The Scene

There are also some exciting new additions to the attitude-changing movies of the 1970's. New on the scene are personalities who are actively counseling thousands regarding the realities of this new unseen world. And those ghost horror shows of our youth don't seem to be following us under the bed covers anymore. Our attitudes toward the unseen world have shifted from a state of fear to a willingness to explore what's out there. Many of us even seem anxious to embark upon new adventures, adventures that cross old boundaries of fear and superstition and lead to discoveries of other dimensions of reality.

And it is appearing that the unseen world is not flat, as the ancients thought of the earth. There is roundness and dimension and unlimitedness, and beauty and peace and love; all those things that we know are there but somehow have been unreachable to us. This *Voyage To The New World* then, is your ticket to hop onto a fun ride—riding your attitudes into the ·infiniteness of the unseen world. And what does that mean? You, as the adventurer, will develop an omniscient wisdom, a complete understanding of life. You will complete the story of your life into a discovery of the majesty of you. And for what result? The manifestation of your dreams and desires. And once your dreams and desires are completely satisfied, you will be living in the unlimited world of your dreams.

Voyage To The New World is an adventure book about many people and their many lives. You will read questions of the most intimate nature, questions of fun and delight, questions about death, questions about life. You will be astounded about the answers as your contemporary knowledge data banks fill with new information not previously heard on this planet. By simply allowing your mind the unlimited adventure of pure, unaltered thought, you can sail into the heights of forever.

Fiction Or Non-fiction

Is this book fiction or non-fiction? Could it reflect both illusion and reality? And, what is illusion and what is reality—because something can't be seen, does that make it an illusion? How do you explain electricity? Electricity is a reality even though it can't be seen. In fact, all of us are sustained by a reality that can't be seen—oxygen. To many, unseen worlds are an everyday reality. To many, thoro io no fiction—if something can be thought, it is, it exists. In the early twentieth century, electricity was only just a thought. Today, it remains an unseen reality that benefits us all.

If the vision of an unseen world is beginning to tickle your imagination, you might also want to consider the possibilities of multi-dimensions. Instead of the dimensions that we are familiar with—length, breadth, height, time, space—could there be other dimensions, other realities, other worlds that we don't have the eyes to see but that whirl around us continuously? The blades of a fan inoperative are visible, cold, hard steel. Turn the fan on and the blades disappear into a cool breeze. The blades are now manifesting in another dimension. Caution, don't stick your finger in!

And here's another one for you to ponder. If there are other places that exist beyond our sight, could our souls be unlimited enough to live in those other dimensions at the *same* time that they live in this seen world of planet Earth, year 1987? If this is the case, if our souls can occupy unseen worlds, how do we beam-in to those worlds? Perhaps unlimited adventures are only a thought away? Perhaps allowing an unlimited thought to carry you to another dimension is the ticket to an eternity of adventure.

Many are beginning to believe that all of these unseen realities are quite possible because they are beginning to understand how they have created their own reality in *this* earth-bound world. They are discovering that it was their attitude that has and *is* creating their reality. I have a friend who placed this sign outside of his office door, "DO NOT DISTURB — I am creating my own reality." Many are concluding that they have written the plot of their life through their attitude. And they are finding out that every instant, in a waking state or in a sleeping state, shapes their thinking. And *every* thought shapes their attitude.

The missing link to this progression is described in this book. The missing link is, *every* thought and *every* word manifests into a reality. And time is *not* a factor in this manifestation process. Whatever you think and speak is on hold, if you will, and *will* manifest in the next instant, or in your next lifetime, or in your lifetimes to come. This manifesting process is only part of the gift of your birthright. So, quite possibly, there is no such thing as fiction. Quite probably, all thoughts eventually create their own world of non-fiction.

A Most Entertaining Entertainment Channel

*I am Ramtha, The Enlightened
One,* totally. *And who I be
I love you greatly. This hour we
will open books and see and
ponder and engage and enlighten
and expand, and you all will be
exceedingly glad for it. So be it!*

After these words, a male entity who calls himself Ramtha, The Enlightened One, proceeds to discourse, mimic, laugh, teach and enlighten a gathering numbering in the hundreds. Those who have gathered are business people, politicians, entertainers, thinkers and doers, decision-makers asking Ramtha about the issues of this planet and of their lives. Ramtha teaches, advises, satisfies, inspires, captivates, deliberates, challenges and tantalizes. Ramtha appears quite grand yet enigmatic in his grandeur as he brings forth significant news for the gathering.

How Does One Explain The Appearance Of An Unseen Person?

Ramtha is, quite possibly, the clearest voice to the unseen world ever to communicate with the seen world. Ramtha appears to be a master counselor who transcends time and space. What is Ramtha, The Enlightened One? Ramtha is an entity who exists in dimensions unknown to us. We live in a seen reality; Ramtha is known to our souls who live in an unseen reality. Ramtha speaks through a woman named J.Z. Knight. J.Z. is a channel into the unseen world. At the time of this publication, Ramtha has delivered approximately one hundred Dialogues. These communications comprise a collection of approximately six hundred cassette tapes, about nine hundred hours of news; new information for the planet.

The first popularized emergence of an unseen personality was the delivery of the *Seth Materials* through the channel Jane Roberts. Published internationally in 1972 by Prentice-Hall, *Seth Speaks* quickly became a bestseller as it explored the realities of the unknown world. Seth was the first unseen entity who was generally accepted by a large readership, numbering in the millions. Prior to Seth, Edgar Cayce, in fourteen thousand documented stenographic records, channeled healing and prophecy to six thousand people over a forty-three year period. Cayce's *Life Readings* are today protected by a foundation and are studied by increasing numbers each year.

Shirley MacLaine's *Out On A Limb*, published by Bantam Books in hardcover and then in mass-market paperback, was one of the biggest bestsellers in the early 1980's. Miss MacLaine's book was the beginning of a whole new genre, books that *crossed-over* for many millions of readers. For the first time in contemporary publishing history, people who would not ordinarily pick up a book about the unseen worlds were reading all about Miss MacLaine's adventures, her search all around the globe for explanation and reason in life. Miss MacLaine also won the Best Actress Oscar in 1984 for her performance in *Terms of Endearment*. This award brought Miss MacLaine and her books even more attention. Her fourth biography, *Dancing in the Light*, is opening up even grander horizons for her readers.

Alice A. Bailey appeared as a prominent channel in the

1920's. Her first contact with the Tibetan teacher Djwhal Khul [D.K.] was in California in November, 1919. Together, the unseen entity D.K. and Ms. Bailey planned a thirty year activity schedule. She channeled twenty-five books, passing the plane a few months after her *schedule* was complete. In 1888, H.P. Blavatsky, of Russia, channeled the *Secret Doctrine* volumes, two seven-hundred page treatises on cosmogenesis and anthropogenesis, the birth of the cosmos and the birth of man. Even though they were well known, these volumes were very difficult to understand because of the technical nature of their terminology. Various study groups developed to help with the interpretation.

Channeling is not new to this planet; however, the *acceptability* of channeling *is* new. Two major treatises have acquired international renown—*A Course In Miracles,* published in 1975 and now in its eighth printing, is a one thousand page channeling which explains the manifestation tools of the miracle of life; and *The Urantia Book,* published in 1955, now in its seventh printing, is a two thousand page compilation of papers sponsored by Counselors in the Unseen which discusses the various universes, the history of the earth, and the life and teachings of Jesus the Christ.

All of these unseen personalities, through their channels, have brought forth new wonderments of knowledge. Yet, the emergence of Ramtha differs from the others—he is the first to appear before large gatherings in scheduled appearances. The significance of these *personal* appearances is many-faceted, not the least being credibility: Ramtha stands behind what he says, and what he says has become a visible reality for all to see. Over seven thousand people have attended Ramtha's personal appearances.

Caution: Followship May Be Hazardous To Your Self

One word of caution before you begin your adventure. There are many situations in today's world that ask of you worship. Religions specifically demand that you worship their particular lord. Self-help programs specifically demand that you worship the particular visions of their particular lord who has created their particular program. The paradox is that all self-help programs and religions flourish because of the specific pretense that they will help you find your *Self*. Yet, many end up lost because they were taught to find their Self through the idolatry of another via the process of followship.

The role of worship is the role of followship: following the greatness of someone or something else. In following the greatness of another, one tends to overlook the greatness in one's Self. Worship experiences are, however, a necessary step that eventually lead you to your own brand of Self. The follower in a followship may eventually discover that he is worshipping everything except his *own* Self. This voyage that you are about to embark upon is not a voyage captained by followship. This is a voyage on your Self-ship, captained by you.

Bon Voyage!

*I am Ramtha, The Enlightened
One. Whatever you do not know,
whatever you need, you will have.
Whatever you want you will
have, for then you are no longer
enslaved to want, to desire and
need, and ignorance. We do this
first for this wondrous gathering,
and give unto you whatever you
are needing, whatever your
desire, whatever be good for you,
as it were, in this wondrous
moment. And when you are filled
with that we will fill you with
more.*

Ramtha, One On One

In order to channel the personality Ramtha, J.Z. Knight's
Soul leaves her body. According to J.Z., this *leaving* experience appears to be similar to those who have experienced
the Soul passing to another plane of existence via an astral
excursion. J.Z.'s *leaving* also appears to be similar to the
"death" experiences reported by those who have medically
died and who have returned to life via an unusual set of circumstances.

Just before J.Z. leaves her body, she begins to raise the
vibrations of her Soul so she can meet Ramtha at his
vibratory level. The next sensation she is aware of is moving down a corridor similar to a hall or a tunnel. Gathering
speed she travels toward a light which becomes larger and
larger and larger. Her face feels like it is being stretched by
an exceptional gravitational force—that force takes her
breath away. The instant she enters that light, her Soul has
emerged from out of her body and the essence of Ramtha

15

appears in her place. The essence of J.Z. has transcended to another time and space, another dimension.

When Ramtha begins his appearance in the embodiment of J.Z. Knight, a completely different sensation from that of J.Z.'s embodiment is felt. The body of J.Z. Knight is still present but a totally different personality emerges—her body seems larger and stronger, bursting at the seams; the softness of J.Z.'s mannerisms and facial expressions are replaced by those of a man; body postures and gestures are surging with power; his concentration becomes an intensity, the voice is that of another knowingness.

You are about to begin your voyage. This book will present to you an unlimited passageway into the unseen world of your unlimited realities. Within your Soul exists the book of you. Therein are contained your memory banks—the floppy discs of your past, present, and future—known collectively as your Isness. All that you have been, felt, and thought is available to Ramtha. He simply selects the volume he wishes, opens it and begins his communication.

The words of Ramtha are lush in their impressions, vivid in their dreams, magical in their moments. These words will tingle your Soul, they might awaken you to the remembrance of your birthright. And for what purpose are words but to remind you of the divinity that you are. Fasten your seat belt for this psychic exploration into the vastness of Self.

And J.Z. Signs Off . . .

"From the essence of my being to the essence of all of your beings, I love you, I value highly your presence here. I know that you will be enlightened by the enlightened one. I will see you again when I return. So be it."

Anticipatory stillness fills the hall. Someone moves, a chair creeks. J.Z. closes her eyes. Everyone watches and waits. J.Z.'s chin drops slowly . . . her breathing becomes slow and deep, then louder; then masculine strength boldly appears in her body, stretches his legs one at a time, shoes loudly impacting the floor like a seasoned sea captain pacing on deck challenging a storm. He adjusts his chair with a jolt. His eyes open in certainty, he steadfastly scans the gathering. And then he proclaims . . .

"I am Ramtha, The Enlightened One, indeed."

The entity who calls himself Ramtha, The Enlightened One, has completely appropriated the body of J.Z. Knight. Enjoy it as perhaps one of the most fascinating experiences of your life.

SECRETS
FROM
THE
SOUL

FORGOTTEN YET KNOWN

ANCHORS AWEIGH!

*Are you a lover of magicians? All
are lovers of genies and magicians.
They do not love them for
themselves; they love them for
what they can do for them. All
that you need we shall provide
for, to help you understand. And
you will enjoy it and revel in it
whatever it be. But all through it
you will learn from these things
given to you and it will teach you
and refine you to be better and
more brilliant and more superb.*

My Most Illustrious Brotheren

RAMTHA I am Ramtha, The Enlightened One, indeed. And
who be I, as it were? I be that which is termed indeed,
servant unto God Almighty, that which is called The Principle Cause, The Light Force, The Element, that which is
termed The Spirit, that which is conclusive all of Itself,
that which is termed The All in All, that which is called
Life, indeed.

I am Ramtha, The Enlightened One, indeed! Servant unto
that which is termed the Christus. And who be he, as it
were? To the Father who be termed The Principle Cause,
The Source, The Element, The Giver of All that Be—unto
that which is termed All That Is, there came an expansion
of that which is called contemplative thought of His most
superlative being. In order to have expanded parts of His
being, the Father contemplated and extended Himself Into
a uniqueness of form. From The Source came the Perfect
Expanded Part of The Father, The Source, The Element.
The Understanding of the Singular Active Participant of

21

the Source be called the Perfect Son, The Ideal, The Perfect
Reflector, The Inherited Entity of All that the Father was.

Unto It, the expanded parts from The Father, came The
Son blessed of all that be; Singularly Evolving Thought,
Understanding confined to one movement. The Movement
of the Father became the Son, and what the Son accom-
plishes the Father has accomplished. The Son became in
his ideal form and in his creative cause that which is
termed Man. The Son be called Christ. Son/God; God/Man;
Man/God. That which is termed The Beloved Father
expressive unto The Christ Realized am I a servant unto
this hour.

Who Be You?

I am Ramtha, the Enlightened One, indeed. And who be
you, my most illustrious brotheren, who have gathered
yourselves into this wondrous audience? You be that which
is termed Man, you be that which is termed Christus, you
be that which is termed God. Fallacy? Reality! You be of
your importance and your value and your word far greater
than that which you have first concluded yourself to be.
You be the totality of all that The Father is: God Supreme.
What else be there? What grander a state is there?

You, my beloved brotheren, illustrious of your cause,
designers of your destiny, you be important and valued
and loved above all kingdoms, greater than all kingdoms.
The Soul of your being, the contemplative thought co-
creativeness of your being, is a most wondrous thing. You,
who have thought yourself to be destitute, to be [only] of
yourselves, to be without, worthless, not having importance, demeanor, character, zest of exuberance for living,
you be God.

Who Be I?

Wondrous entities, beloved brotheren—I am a servant
unto you, for you be unto me, indeed, lover of my being and

I be of yours. I am a servant unto each of you who are gathered in this wondrous structure, in this wondrous place. You have gathered yourselves here for I who love you need to give unto you that which is termed the meagerness of my wondrous teachings. And to enlighten you and to expand your thinking into greater vastness. And to give unto you what is called a great opportunity to become the highest of your perfected, elevated Self.

And who be I? Your servant, your teacher this hour, your beloved brother. Unto me worship not for I shall not worship you. Unto this hour let us put forth the most wondrous of ideals; to gather ourselves up into a most wondrous expedition for the pursuit of exploration and adventure. And all that are gathered here will learn from me who loves you to be the greatest and the height of your being, for you will learn from me to be a light unto all of your life, unto all of your illusions, unto all of your realities.

For What Purpose?

When love is realized—and *ah*, it is a wondrous word called love, indeed—when *love* is realized and understood, and when the totality, the essence, and the beauty of your wondrous beings [are] realized and understood, you will find that love in its wild and free-moving essence hath for itself a purpose for good within each of you gathered around us, and to the world as you would term it.

And for those who are groping in the enslavement of their darkness, their ignorance, their not-knowing—to give unto them that which is termed hope. Hope—wondrous word! For love is the giver of hope. I give unto you hope this hour for you to become all that you are and intended to be beyond the expanse of your limited territorial boundaries, that you may love others to the degree that The Father has loved you, to become all things in your designs as you have seen them.

A Coming Upon This Plane

There be upon this plane a coming which is called The Close of Your Time. Upon this closing there will be an opening into a Great Age. You have called this age by various names and forms but it shall be called and rendered to The Age of God—The Age of Pure Spirit. This is your Age of Reckoning, the settling of accounts; that is coming unto the close of what has been called The Age of Flesh. Flesh is as wondrous, too—it be God; to be experienced, to be loved.

But the *greater* giver of all gifts, including that which is termed The Flesh, is the Beloved Spirit—the Beloved God of your Wondrous Beings. The Age that is upon you is The Age of God, The Age of Spirit. And all who enter therein unto the times and the time that is coming be termed The Reckoning Within The Spirits of Their Being. Here are the Lovers of the Word, the Thought, the Good.

The Lessness Of Your Reckoning

You know there is much fear connected with this coming. It is created by only those who wish to enslave you, [who] wish to keep you from your joyfulness and your happiness. The Age that is coming is Life—Ongoingness; the greater, more perfectedness of life. We are preparing you so you will understand this a bit better. And for that we will all be exceedingly glad.

Worth and Value, Participant of Life, that what you be, you are my beloved brethren. You be unequivocally God! You say you are tired of hearing the word? Never tire of hearing the word; you cannot say it nearly enough. God be you that be all encompassing. God be you and the totality of your worth and your value. Do not reckon yourself less for if you do you will become the lessness of your reckoning.

The Business Of This Audience

Now that *that* is understood let us get on with this business of audience this day in your time. That which is termed knowledge be the giver of understanding. When one hath this knowledge he hath that which is termed his staff. His staff can be to him as a kingdom is to a king. Let them take away the kingdom but as long as the king has the knowledge and the good sense of his understanding with him, he can build yet another. It is your standing lot.

In the hour to come in your time, knowledge, enlightenment, understanding, truth as it is so seen this hour, shall be given unto you as the Lord God of my Perfect Being shall manifest it for you. For you be the believers and the livers on a reality that is called Three Dimensional, Three Understanding, Three Space. And all that truth shall come to pass so you may reckon yourselves with it. That *is*; it is no longer philosophy or wondrous words. Let it become a profound truth for you to expand your creative thoughts for.

The great whore, as it were—Fear—enslaves, encaptures and inhibits the creative mind. It does not permit love to bloom in its wondrous fields; it does not permit life to be reveled upon; it stagnates the emotions and kills hope. Fear is born out of not-knowingness: whatever you are in not-knowingness of you are enslaved to, you are in darkness about. This hour shall bring not-knowingness forth in the clarity of our wondrous light, to pursue it and find all the answers that have kept us in the state of not-knowingness. And then we are freed! Do we not have dominion over not-knowingness once again? Indeed we do. God be you: you have dominion over all of your kingdoms and principalities.

Whatever you do not know, whatever you need you will have. Whatever you want you will have for then you are no longer enslaved to want nor desire nor need nor ignorance. We do this first for this wondrous audience; give unto you whatever you are needing, whatever you desire, whatever be good for you in this wondrous moment. And when you are filled with that we will fill you with more, whatever you need and want and desire. And when you are filled with that, we will give you yet more and more and more.

Now, what of material values? They are not blasphemous things as some would have you to know. Are they not The Father? All things in The Light Force are in Thought. And all things that are are God, even your gold, your rubies, your exchange; whatever you wish to term them it still be God. And one cannot curse one form and love another and be pious in doing so. Man must love all that is around him for all that is around him be The Source, The Father, The Principle Understanding, The Giver of All Creativeness.

When one learns to understand whatever his need, be it gold or shelter or food stuffs, it is given. For it is God that is the Giver—the Good to which all things are made up of. And once you are contented entities no longer enslaved to the *I wants*, when you have all that you want, then we give unto you the understanding of who is the true giver of these and how the science comes into play.

Once you understand this you will not have time for your thoughts of boredom, your thoughts of selfishness or pity; of anxiety, fear, gloom, worry, sorrow, despair, war, diseasements. You will have no time for this for you will be caught up in the gloriousness of expanded creativity that is ever-moving, that is ever-ongoing. You do not have the time as you would allot yourselves, not even on this plane, to sit and contemplate the despair of some forgotten moment that has no bearing upon the principle Now.

You will not be bored; you will be God. The more you give, the more you receive. The more you receive through expanded creative thought, the more you become the giver. And when you become the giver, you will become the element—the Moon Enchantress in her light; the perfume of a sweet flower; the wonders of an insect and its color; the mysterious thought of the fish; the light of your dawn; the sweetness and laughter of the child; and a woman's wonderful hips, and hair and love, for you will become the All-Essence that is—The Allness.

And once you are there you will become what we are setting out here this hour in this wondrous audience to achieve. We start by first understanding and giving knowledge, and then through that knowledge we see the advancement of it, and then we become it. And that we do now!

Are You A Lover Of Magicians?

All are lovers of genies and magicians. They do not love them for themselves; they love them for what they can do for them. All that you need we shall provide for, to help you understand. And you will enjoy it and revel in it whatever it be. But all through it you will learn from these things given to you and it will teach you and refine you to be better and more brilliant and more superb.

My beloved audience. You are gathered here looking upon my beautiful daughter and find that I am an enigma. Perhaps you will curse me and smirk me, whatever it is it does not matter. But I wish you to listen. For when you listen you will learn to give unto yourselves the opportunity to advance yourselves. And when you listen to the truth that be given you, you will feel and understand the love that also be given. That *love* will make your life in the grandest sort more extensive and more beautiful and more fulfilled.

I am Ramtha, The Enlightened One, totally! And who I be I love you greatly. This hour we will open books and see and ponder and engage and enlighten and expand and you all will be exceedingly glad for it. So be it.

TRUTH COME FORTH! Truth be abating upon us. Open forth indeed the wondrous parts of your being that all is seen and known. Let the word be the action; let the action be the form; let the form be representative of the God that is within us all. And unto this hour truth, let it be given unto The Father, unto The Source, into the primal understanding that all be one to that glory and to that beauty and to that ongoingness of perfect life, for [that] we are all in servants to. So be it.

Let us begin. Wondrous audience, as it were. There are so many curious hearts. Where shall we begin? [A short pause] I shall begin my audience this hour with you.

Your Prayers And Your Desires Have Been Heard

RAMTHA Beloved woman who sits in front of my being most nervously, you may look upon my countenance, Entity, I will not turn you into a frog. I am pleased that you have come here. Let us get on with answering the questions. What desire you?

MASTER Well, I had about a hundred questions but I couldn't sort them out, so I decided just to ask you what I need to know now, if you could tell me, just to keep me moving.

RAMTHA [You need to know] everything that you don't know and have not permitted yourself to experience, for if you knew more than you would allow yourself to experience you would not be in your predicament. Now, Lass, what is it that you need to know? What ideal could you be that, if you could be that, would know everything there is to know about you? Who would that entity be?

MASTER Me.

RAMTHA Ah, well, so how define you the term *you*? Well, you're greater than your body because your thought can reach the sun in a moment. Or [your thought] can pierce within their own cells of a hundred universes within a universe to try to find you. But you are a collection of all that is, Lass. The difficulty is that you reach certain points in your life and you learn all there is to learn during that time but you are fearful of going on to the next step. You have a difficulty with being very secure. Now, what would happen if you were insecure all the time, aye? Would you continue to live?

MASTER I feel like I *am* insecure all the time.

RAMTHA Well, have you progressed from when you were a little girl up until this hour as a woman still being insecure. Have you still managed to live?

MASTER Yes.

RAMTHA Ah, then you are not so insecure after all.

MASTER No, no I'm not.

RAMTHA Well, what would you like to change about yourself if you could change anything, Entity who is you?

MASTER I would like to change my resistance to knowing the things that scare me; to know about myself, my . . . I'm afraid to know so it's painful, so I have to get off of it.

RAMTHA Ah, well, there I will help you. I will manifest all your fears for you—everything!

MASTER I think you're a little late. [Audience joins in her laughter]

29

RAMTHA   They only remain a fear, Entity, when you do not know about them. If you know about them they are no longer a fear.

MASTER   Yes, that's what I'm afraid of.

RAMTHA   What I shall do with you is I shall bring two people from your past that have been very instrumental in causing this inferiorness within your being. I will bring them to you straightaway. Now, the others, Entity, I bring forth from the depths of your being and they shall come forth and they shall ride the sea of your Entity until they reach the shore of knowingness.

I will manifest all your fears, all of your unworthiness, all of your lackings, all of your insecurities about you in this your year to come—everything. Now, my master, you will think it's funny when we have gotten through all of them for then you will have seen how unmeaningful they have been in your life. We shall do it straightaway.

Now do remember this, you are going to live through all of this so nothing is so great as is going to take your life. You have managed to live all this time so you're not so bad as you once thought you were. We do that, Lass, and you're going to grow strong and beautiful and fervent within your character. The womenness of your being will emerge and the beauty of your being will emerge, and you will make peace with the two and your life, Entity, and a glow [will emerge] that you have not even fathomed within your own thought, and that will come.

Lass, you know, you cannot love other entities

until you've learned to love yourself, for who is
due to find love grander than the entity giving
it. If he knows not what [love] is for his *own*
Self, indeed, how can he give it to others? 'Tis
the same with you. In learning to love yourself
is to deny others until such time you have come
to terms with *you* and have found that all that
you are evokes passion and beauty and ecstasy
within your own being. Never have you done
these things before for you have thought
yourself unworthy, unbeautiful, unwanted most
of your beautiful life.

You are going to learn how to love that which is
termed Self and I will send you the runners
that will be nearest you to help you. And once
you learn to do that, wondrous Entity, then you
will have the capacity to love those that are
around you and understand yourself to a
greater degree. And never again will you ever
ask the opinion of anyone what think they of
you for it does not matter. Do you understand?

MASTER   Yes I do.

RAMTHA   Beloved lady, you are loved greatly. And that
which is termed your prayers and your desires
have been heard. And all of them will be
answered this year within your understanding
as you know it. So be it. And one day you will
fancy yourself peering at yourself in that which
is termed a reflector and you will find that you
look most wondrous to your being for you will
have a peace in your being, Entity, that does
passeth all understanding. For you, that is the
greatest thing that I can give to you.

MASTER   Yes.

RAMTHA   I will tend to it straightaway. So be it.

An Open And Shut Gate

RAMTHA   Beloved entity who gaze upon [me] with wondrous eyes. What desire you?

MASTER   I would like to know why I seem to restrict myself and seem to close myself at times when at other times I think of myself as being very open?

RAMTHA   You are like a gate, are you not?

MASTER   I guess. I never thought of it like that.

RAMTHA   Well, think of it that way because that is how you are. You open when you want to open and you close when you want to close.

MASTER   That's true. That's true.

RAMTHA   Now, who is to say that that which is termed progress is not achieved being closed?

MASTER   It's not always a comfortable closing though.

RAMTHA   It never is when you are criticized for being that way. Master, you are a God; you are a God who possesses that which is termed an ego that is altered—*altered* meaning it is altered God. Altered God means incomplete God to that which is termed the understanding that full knowledge, that which you are, has been arrested in this life. But everyone else suffers that also.

Alteredness also means that you have formulated opinions or collective attitudes. Collective attitudes are buried and impressed upon the Soul and [when] impressed upon the Soul give quality to that which is termed

thoughts that emerge through the auric field,
through the central nervous system and are
recorded through the Soul—that gives
reasoning. Much of [what] that which is termed
your opinions have been based on has not
permitted you to open the gate because you
keep it closed because of fear. Indoctrination of
that which is termed opinions are based on fear.

Contemplate this for a moment. You only ask
someone else's opinion because you fear that
which you are is not acceptable, and they
reassure you. That is only a minute example,
but opinions are based through fear. Thus, the
attitudes that you have accumulated have shut
the gate and not allowed you to progress
because of that which is termed the basis of
fear. That is altered God. Altered God
possesses fear and knows a reality of it. God-
ego without that which is termed alterations
knows no fear and goes beyond that which is
termed the fear into unlimitedness. They open
the gate very wide for all that passeth are in
the scheme of understanding within its Soul.

You are not unlike anyone else, Entity. The
reason it stays shut is that you are fearful of
allowing it to be open. It's disarming when one
has himself figured out pretty well in his
attitudes and that which is termed figured out
very well, to have to open them to the attitudes
of someone else and lose your identity. That is
what troubles the whole plane. Now, you wish a
littlo holp?

MASTER Yes I do.

RAMTHA I will blow open your gate. Being here with me,

Entity, was quite an opening for not everyone believes as I am. That is all right, it does not really matter. What really matters is the treasure they obtain from it, and I give you a treasure.

You contemplate that which I have told you. You will advance you greatly. And one other thing; unlimited thought, Entity, is the pathway into the Kingdom of Heaven. Thought is the Father Manifest; the *feeling* is the reality of the Thought felt by each individual entity. The one sovereign Thought may have completely different effects on everyone in one same area because they feel it differently. That is their sovereign right to do so, but the greater the unlimited thought, the greater it is to become. *Becoming* means to become unaltered.

In The Wilderness Of God

Go beyond, Entity. Transcend that which is termed accepted moral, accepted ideal, accepted society, accepted rule. Go beyond where genius lies, only in the outside of the perimeter, and wallow in it, Entity. Then you are in the wilderness of God. Then, Master, you are taken up and never will you return, and it is ever so short in getting through. You only have to say, "What if it were so; what if what I hear is a reality, for if I hear it, certainly it is based upon the premise of reality. So thus it is."

Remember, all truth—there is nothing but it. There is no such thing as untruth or lie, there is only truth [and] the degrees in which it is displayed. Allow that which is termed the flourishing of a greater kingdom to yet behold in your future. Be pleased with who and what you are. But never be afraid of losing yourself, Master, for you never will. So be it.

Now, you gaze with your wondrously cerulean blue eyes into the beauty that lies within your nest and when you see alteredness or fear, Entity, call it forward. Let it be dealt with. Then you are going to see an evenness within your Soul that will rejoice you forever. So be it. You need a little help on some direction. I will send you a runner who will help you with it. So be it. You are greatly loved.

Self-Love Is Where World-Love Begins

RAMTHA Master, what say you indeed?

MASTER I think, more than anything else at the moment, I want to feel Self-worth and have more confidence to express myself.

RAMTHA So be it. Know you why you would not express Self-worth and confidence before in your time, as you reckon it?

MASTER I'm trying to.

RAMTHA Humanity is very rigorous and it is very demanding, and they oftentimes do not open and allow themselves to be receptive to soft entities because of very unfeeling realities called survival. So the little entities are rushed up into the wave, thrown against the rocks.

The reason you do not have Self-confidence, Master, is that you want to be loved. Loving—always it is taught here to be loved outside of your Self, never *to* your Self; that is indicative of being selfish. Well, I would rather have the lot of you be *Self-ish* for Self-love is where world-love begins. Wanting to be loved you will put on any image, do anything necessary to gain the admiration and that which is termed the fickle opinion of those that are around you because that equates you are being loved and that you are important.

Well, you are going to learn about *Self*-love. No one around you is worth sacrificing yourself to—they will never die for you and they really do not care what you do, only when it necessitates helping them. When you learn that this whole world and everyone in this wondrous room are really living for themselves and not you, then you will ask yourself, "Who, alas, am I worth living for?" [and you will hear] "Me!" And then that which is termed the *I Am* takes upon that which is termed a wondrous picture to do and to go about and entertain itself however it wishes to. Start doing what you want to do.

You know, God is everything—He is every *thing*. So *any* thing you do, you have an inner action in divinity. Remember that, and do what you want to do, and portray yourself how you want to portray yourself, and let the world alone. Then you will learn to love yourself and this I will help you with straightaway. So be it.

The Pain Allows The New Dawn To Come

And if you were not here you would have been sorely missed, Lass. You love yourself, that I will teach you how to do. It will take a little time to learn it, and it will have pain with it.

But the pain allows the new dawn to come, and that we will do straightaway.

Now, your family, you have been separated. I [will] bring them closer to you. I [will] let you see them, how they really are, and of that which you have been indifferent to and could not come to terms with, I am going to bring the herald of peace, there will be a reckoning there. You are going to find that that which is termed the evenness of your being is going to rejoice this year for you will have eyes to see what is really there. So be it. You are worth loving, Lass. Desire you anything else?

MASTER Peace.

RAMTHA Oh, that! Everyone utterly fails to recognize that peace is a self-ordained act. You will have a lot of that when you become *self*-ordained. So be it. You're greatly loved and you listen this day, Entity, and you will learn a great deal. So be it.

Be Happy You Are The Way You Are

RAMTHA Master, indeed.

MASTER I would like to know why I don't have very strong desires? Whether I have something or don't have something doesn't really matter to me.

RAMTHA Because it doesn't really matter to you!

MASTER Well then, what do I desire in life?

RAMTHA To be desireless. Lass, there is nothing wrong with that at all. I will tell you why. Most that are filled with unquenchable desires never know

who they are for they are too busy wanting.
When you realize that everything you want is
within you, then the source brings a treasure at
your doorstep and leaves it there every moment
of being. And you have everything you ever
wanted—*you*. What you have, many should
have. You're suffering a neurosis for you feel
you should have all of these things, and they
are suffering a neurosis for they want all of
them. Be happy you are the way you are for
[that] means that [the entity] is happy with
itself, and you certainly have most reason to be
that way.

To be desireless does not mean that you are an
uncreative entity. You are a most creative
entity. Your pleasure comes in daydreams and
wonderful imaginations. What greater treasure
is that, for you have the freedom to exist and to
be and to act however you wish for that is God
exerting itself within the perimeters you've
allowed it to. One day we shall break the
perimeters, that all of your imaginations come
to a wonderful pass within your life. [And why
do you not have strong desires?] Of other
existences, you've gotten everything you really
wanted before. In this life you are going to
learn to live now.

Allow The Belief To Occur That Is Magic

I am pleased you have come forth. A fortnight
from this day you are going to need my help,
Entity. I will help you. Go out into that which
is termed the air and call me forth. I will come
from a wind from nowhere and I will help you
with that which you need. And when it is all
said and done I desire for you to thank the God

that lies within you for allowing the belief to
occur that is magic. So be it.

All That The Father Desires From Anyone Is Happiness

MASTER I require, I desire clarity, specifically in what is
my next profession area, clarity in my
relationships, clarity in my Self-expression.

RAMTHA Where shall we begin?

MASTER Profession.

RAMTHA Of course. Clarity. What does that word mean
to you?

MASTER A certainty that is within the realm of peace. I
don't have a necessity to seek a certainty but I
want a knowingness that I'm at peace with,
that I feel good about.

RAMTHA [A knowingness] that makes you happy.

MASTER Yes!

RAMTHA My beloved master. I will tell you, know what
the destiny of your Father that is All Things
desires for You, which is He, to be?

MASTER Is that a question?

RAMTHA It is indeed!

MASTER Everything that I can be.

RAMTHA What does *can* mean?

MASTER Everything that I am, whether or not known.

RAMTHA Happiness. All that the Father that is All
Things desired for anyone was never law but
happiness. Now, your profession should not be

39

based upon law or based upon that which is termed family traditions or society's demand. It should be based upon what desire you to do in the moments of your existence that brings joy, for truly searched for, Entity, they bring the gold. But that is only secondary; the primary is happiness—what you can labor at that is joyful. Now, what desire you to do that makes you happy?

MASTER Teach!

RAMTHA And why does that make you happy?

MASTER I don't know. It's more of an experience than a knowing. It's an experience here, [in my Soul]. But to answer the question, because it serves; I feel I serve when I teach.

RAMTHA Who is really being served when one teaches?

MASTER The teacher.

RAMTHA Indeed! Now, Teacher, what desire you to learn?

MASTER My relationship with God and my Godliness.

RAMTHA That is a most noble request and your whole life depends upon it. That is what you call clarity. So be it. We bring you to the point of clear knowingness and understanding about the nucleus of your being. I will exalt you and make you a teacher. So be it. You are greatly loved.

It Is Not Your Right To Try To Make Anyone Else Happy

RAMTHA Now, let us get on with relationship clarity. What mean relationship clarity unto you?

MASTER Happiness.

RAMTHA Of course. On their part or yours?

MASTER On all parts.

RAMTHA That is very difficult and very selfish, Entity,
and enslaving on your part, for who are you to
demand that everyone be happy? Your concept
of happiness will never be the concept of
another's happiness. Thus in the relationship it
has become singular. Now we are back to God.
So be it. That has already been answered—next.

MASTER I'm not sure that I understand . . .

RAMTHA If you cannot make anyone else happy, nor is it
your right to try to do so, Entity, then the
teacher is all that is left and his happiness, and
that has already been answered.

MASTER Ah, yes.

RAMTHA Ah!

Even The Paint That Is Upon Their Face Owns Them

RAMTHA Do continue, Master.

MASTER I desire an end to financial pressure.

RAMTHA You will never have enough, there will never be
an end to it.

MASTER The pressure?

RAMTHA You know, as long as that which is termed
financial difficulties exist and finances are the
priority in one's life, he is never without it and
he never will be for he has chosen that as his
destiny. How you release yourself from financial

41

pressures is to release the things that are the
catalyst to the pressure. They are not worth
your suffering or the stress of your
unhappiness. Nothing is. The greatest joy a
teacher has with the God within his being is to
be owned by nothing, and you are owned by
everything. Most in this room are—even the
paint that is upon their face owns them.

Now, I will take away your pressures. But I'm
going to remove the things that cause it the
most and though, as it were indeed, you will
curse me, you will love me for what I will do
and then you will be free. Then you will
understand what God is within his own being.
And that powerful creative all-knowing, wise,
intelligence that you shall become, Entity,
creates the enigma gold all around you.

Everyone here serves for the pence and they
serve for that which is termed the gold; it never
has served *them*. When they learn to be the
Lord God of their Totality they have dominion
over everything and, alas, what is left of a man
when you strip everything away from him? His
noble virtue which should never be taken. And
the only way it is ever seen is when he is in the
midst of freedom. You are going to learn about
that which is termed noble virtue, Entity,
because you want to become a teacher. You will
not be in abstinence poverty; no one who loves
the God that they are ever is. But you are
going to be free from that which is termed
awesome enslavement that many are enslaved
to. So be it.

I work the wonder straightaway. So be it. I am
pleased you have come forth, you have taught

many and *that* is clarity! Desire you anything
else?

MASTER   I desire a teacher/partner that I identify with
more wholly than I have.

RAMTHA   So be it. I will send you your *Self!* You are
greatly loved.

Where All The Truth Known To You Lies

RAMTHA   Master, what say you?

MASTER   Well, most of the questions I had you've
already answered.

RAMTHA   Wondrous woman, what has happened to your
tresses upon your head? They are in a profusion
of disorder.

MASTER   God gave that to me.

RAMTHA   It is very beauteous on your being.

MASTER   Thank you. I'd like to know how one—myself
mainly, I'm sure other people have the same
problem—how do you stop the thoughts and
find the silence inside?

RAMTHA   That is a misconception, Lass. That is a
religious doctrine. You never stop Thought.
Thought is the premise of the Spark of Life.
Each Thought that enters your auric field
enters from that which is termed the receiver or
that which you call the brain. [The brain] is
activated when one of the [Thoughts] that you
are [causes an] open[ing] and receptiv[ity] flows
through.

As [the] hormone flows through that which is
called the pituitary to the pineal and sends an

electrical current through the entire central
nervous system, that actually sends the spark
of life unto that which is termed a minute cell
that interacts and causes the DNA spring to
tighten and then to reproduce itself in a cloning
process called that which is termed the sixth
chromosome within man.

Without Thought, Entity, you cannot live.
Many have taught to still the mind and have no
Thought, that peace exists. There is no such
place as nothingness. Thought, Entity, is even
the space that holds your planets up in the sky
as it does. It is a space, a void that reaches all
one hundred universes. You have been taught
incorrectly, you have pondered incorrectly—you
cannot cease the Thought.

To Bring Peace In

How you bring peace in is to allow the
Thoughts to flow through your being through
Contemplative Thought. They will flow through
your being, interact with the entire Self, bring
about that which is termed splendid memory on
the Soul and allow [you], in a breathtaking
moment, to be creative; that will formulate your
destiny in the next moment to come.

Peace, Entity, is knowing that there are no
restraints. Peace, Entity, is knowingness that
the Thought is allowing life to be. Peace,
Entity, exhibits itself without that which is
termed the alteredness of negativity, evil or
ungood. Peace is knowing that everything that
is felt is purposeful intent. Now, how do you
still your mind? You never will and you never
can. But to allow the Thought to flow through

you will allow the peace to be, for in that moment, Entity, you are in your creative kingdom.

Now, the consciousness that you have been subjugated to, prior to even this audience, has been the Thoughts of others and you have tried to accept them within your own kingdom. Do not try, allow them to flow through. They will flow right out for your own Soul records all the feelings of Thought, and it is therein that it will allow a greater understanding to occur within your being. That which is interacting within you, I shall remove and allow you to understand these words that I have just spoken to you.

You, you are worth reveling in every spark of life that comes to you, and every Thought that comes to you. Contemplation creates wisdom which means you never have to learn it **again**. Do you understand?

MASTER I think so.

RAMTHA You will, but sitting and clearing the mind of all Thoughts—no, you can not do that. For when you are clearing it of all Thoughts, the Thought is, *clearing them out*, so the Thought does remain. Desire you anything else?

MASTER Well, along that same line, is there not a place though, within one's being where there is, well, the place of contemplation. Is that not a place of silence, so to speak, which is the only way I know how to term that?

RAMTHA Master, does a Thought have a sound? Does it have an image?

MASTER Well, it seems like it can.

RAMTHA It only has an image, Entity. Once the Thought is taken into the embodiment and the entire embodiment has felt the sensation, as it were, of the Thought, then the Soul thus records the sensation and the sensation identifies itself as to familiar sensations. Thus it has an image; that is when a Thought is contemplated. A Thought has no reality, it has no purpose for being until it is felt in pure emotion. Emotion gives credence to life, Entity. Words were only created to express the emotion of a Thought that an entity is expressing. It was developed for that which is termed communication, to express divine emotion which is imageless.

Listening To One's Self

Now, the contemplative place of being is being quiet and sitting and listening to the Thoughts that are becoming and the feelings as they rush through your entire being, and how the Soul equates each feeling, whether it is a new sensation that hath no word or it is an old one that aligns with wisdom already learned. That is the contemplative place of that which is termed Divine Self: simply being in a state of *being* one listens to oneself. That is how it is referred to.

You never have to speak a Thought, Entity. It cannot be spoken until it is felt—the *feeling* is the sensation of the Thought. Then you only articulate in the gross sound, but hopefully the sound will equate that which you have within your being. That is how it is. That is the True Science of the Embodiment. That is the True Science of the Spirit. That is the True Science of Thought. Simply think, be and listen to Self. That is where all the answers are, that is where all the wisdom lies, that is where all the truth known to you is. Without thinking you cannot feel; without feeling you cannot express; without expression, Entity, you are hopelessly lost. 'Tis a good thing there is no such thing [as stopping Thought]. Do you understand?

MASTER Yes.

RAMTHA Emotion, laughter, great weeping, *feelings*, Entity, are the truest treasure of experience—not gold or castles or vast mountains or great seas. It is the *feeling* of those things that is the truest treasure. Through Contemplative Thought one is allowed to gather much treasure within his Soul for it is the only thing he can take with him when he leaves this place, the Treasures of Emotions. Learn to be very emotional with what you are feeling. Learn to express it and never be ashamed of it for it is a true creator at work that does so. So be it.

Confusion

RAMTHA What say you, Master?

MASTER I'd like to learn to be less emotional, frankly.

RAMTHA That is being limited.

MASTER I'm teasing.

RAMTHA You're teasing? That is an illusion.

MASTER Well, maybe.

RAMTHA I am pleased you are here.

MASTER Thank you.

RAMTHA Why do you drape yourself in mourning?

MASTER Well, I don't think of it that way.

RAMTHA Let us talk, Lass. What desire you?

MASTER Oh, that's the problem.

RAMTHA There is no such thing as a problem.

MASTER Good! At present, a feeling of more direction. Maybe that's not possible?

RAMTHA Why is that not possible?

MASTER I don't know.

RAMTHA What is impossible?

MASTER Probably nothing.

RAMTHA Nothing is an impossibility. *There* is the only thing there is. Now, let us speak of direction. Where do you want to be?

MASTER Well, that's the problem.

RAMTHA That is not a problem.

MASTER It's not a problem? It's a problem for me.

RAMTHA It will not [be] if you listen. Where would you like to go?

MASTER Well, I've been a lot of places and I guess I have a lot of desires—maybe that's bad, but I do.

RAMTHA No, that is not bad; that means you need them. Is that bad?

MASTER No. No?

RAMTHA Then correct your speech for everything you say, Entity, dictates your tomorrow. Let us get even and speak how it is, aye. Now, you have many desires. Let us talk of your desires and then we shall create direction. So be it. Let us hear them.

MASTER Well, career-wise or personally?

RAMTHA A career is really labor. What would you like to labor at?

MASTER That's the . . . that's . . . I'm in a place now where I'm not sure, I've done so many different things.

RAMTHA What would you like to do?

MASTER What would I like to do?

RAMTHA Indeed. What would bring you happiness?

MASTER I'm not sure. That's the problem—Ah, no problems!

RAMTHA So be it. When you have determined what would make you happy in regards to that which is termed labor, speak it forth, we will open the door. Until *you* know, no one knows, for the divine source shall not give you that which is termed a labor because that is going against your will which is eminent and infinite. When you have determined what desire you, Entity, then that shall be reckoned unto and be given to you. Thus you need to contemplate it. Let us go on to the next.

MASTER Well, you spoke of destiny. Do you see a destiny for me?

RAMTHA Indeed.

[There is a pause]

MASTER Um . . . what?

RAMTHA *Living!*

49

MASTER Oh, well, yes, indeed.

RAMTHA What if you did not, then you would not have these worries of career and desires and labor. I see a wondrous destiny for you, little girl, but it is not in this place, nor is it with the ideas that you are proceeding to have. You do not belong here. Go back to the northern country. There is a great destiny waiting for you.

MASTER Where is the northern country?

RAMTHA Anywhere from this place.

MASTER Are you referring to Los Angeles or the world or . . .

RAMTHA This place. Your city that you live in.

MASTER I don't really live here. That's another thing I wanted to talk about.

RAMTHA Then what are you doing here?

MASTER I'm a gypsy. I'm working here at present.

RAMTHA You're not happy with your labor. What would you like to do?

MASTER Well . . .

RAMTHA Continuing to be a gypsy?

MASTER Well, I've tried to be less of a gypsy. I'm not sure it works.

RAMTHA Were you happy when you became less?

MASTER No.

RAMTHA Then perhaps you should continue to be [a gypsy].

MASTER Uh huh. Where's the northern country?

RAMTHA Washington and Oregon, the Dakota, the Canada and Alaska, a green land.

MASTER Do you see Europe or some other . . . you're shaking your head.

RAMTHA Go away from this place straightaway. Go to the North, wherever your nose leads you. That is where you should be.

MASTER Is New York North? You're shaking your head again. I do very many things and I like parts . . . I like *lots* of things of each one of them and I dislike lots of things about each one of them.

RAMTHA So be it. We will allow you to have that which is termed the things that you love about each of them. And continuing with your way of life, there is nothing wrong with it and there is no problem in it.

MASTER No?

RAMTHA No!

MASTER Also, I'm afraid I . . . I desire entertaining people. I know maybe you're not supposed to but I do and that's the truth.

RAMTHA Everyone wants to do that.

MASTER Do they?

RAMTHA Indeed, and why think you they want to do that?

MASTER I don't know, I don't know what everyone wants, I only know mo.

RAMTHA Then what does "me" want?

MASTER Well, I like the part of that that is the actual

doing. I don't like all of the parts that require you to get to that part.

RAMTHA   Of course, that is uncreative. Most entertain others because it gives them a reference point, that they are something of importance, unique, different—there is nothing wrong with that. There are many who set them[selves] up as idols and wish [all] to be like them. Unfortunately, they never portray the trueness of themselves, only the illusions. Contemplate, Entity, that which is termed doing what you want to do that brings you happiness and go into the northern country. We will open doors for you that you can be able to do what you want to do.

MASTER   Entertain the Eskimos?

RAMTHA   Or perhaps a great bear who would have you for his supper; that would be entertaining, Entity. [Grand laughter] Now, there are marvelous entities that are waiting in the northern lands that are not nearly as critical of your being, nor are they as fickle, a most proper word that I have learned. They are more apt to give you that which is termed an opportunity to do what you want to without criticism and be simply entertained by your wondrous being. And what a wondrous gift to make them laugh and to make them happy. There, Entity, you would be able to do what you wish to do. The great cities that you have mentioned, they are like an old whore—they exalt no one but themselves. You remember that. Go into the land of that which is termed the common peoples'. There you will find a great appreciation of you and [will] learn about you. So be it.

MASTER I don't quite understand what a runner is.

RAMTHA A messenger.

MASTER A relationship; do you see anything?

RAMTHA But not with a bear.

MASTER Darn.

RAMTHA And not with an Eskimo either, with a very good entity. But he is not in this place, he is in the North. [Uproarious laughter] Love always assists everyone in finding out about themselves, and that will be very good for you.

MASTER In the North?

RAMTHA Indeed!

MASTER Thank you.

RAMTHA So be it. Gypsy, aye. I rather like their sort, Entity. We had a whole band of them for a long time in my time.

MASTER Really, when was your time may I ask?

RAMTHA You would call it in your counting thirty-five thousand years ago in your time, at the remains of Lemuria and Atlatia, and when that which is termed the Persian Gulf met that which is termed the African continent. Then a canal separated two main land masses and the ocean was still above the earth.

I had a great army. We went over your world, two thirds of it, and conquered it from tyranny. But I was the greatest tyrant of all in my earlier times. My peoples marched for sixty-three years. That is a great gypsy band, aye? But we learned about God and we learned what the Unknown God was and what the Unknown Peoples were, and perhaps being a gypsy, as you term it, is not so terrible of a thing. Ah, look at all that you learn and all the places you've laid your head, and all the things that you have seen and all the peoples' faces—siblings, warriors, old women, young men. Remember their eyes, they help for you to know yours.

What you are doing I would like all to do in a little way. It would give them a much broader understanding of life, not in the great cities, for that is a cloistered attitude, but in the wilderness. They learn of God's virtue and his Isness and that which is termed their Isness, and no man judge them there. Continue to be a gypsy, Entity. So be it. You have been that which is termed most delightful unto my audience.

The First Priority In Life Is You

RAMTHA Beloved master, what say you?

MASTER I would like to know if there's anything I can do to be a little bit more open and trusting with other people? I've found that very difficult in my lifetime.

RAMTHA There is good reason why. You learn to love all people but you learn to love yourself first, and first meaning, the first priority in life is *you.* Trust is another word for loving Self. If you mistrust anyone there is good reason, for Self is protecting Self. Why should you trust if they have always assailed you? It does not mean that you do not love them. Love everyone and allow them to express however they wish to. But the greater love of Self protects Self from those who otherwise would overtake them and consume them and keep them from allowing Self to interact with Self. It is not really being mistrustful—that is being smart.

Now, many people think that they must stop loving others because they have been mistrustful to them. That is when you are in error, Entity. Never stop loving anyone. And to be a God, infinitely know and understand that they have *their* truth that they are becoming a part of also, and you allow them to do that and never criticize them. Who are you to criticize? But [as you have been], Entity, [you have] opened yourself to be a victim, to be slain by those who would partake [of] you as their truth. Love of Self means to allow them to be but without the interaction with them. You understand?

MASTER Yes, I do.

RAMTHA You know, man is a precarious creature. He has learned to become a herd animal: he cloisters together in great places. The rogue who is the entity who wanders in the wilderness is perhaps the most trustworthy of all, for he has learned to deal with himself and his elements around him and he is a greater understanding of the workings of the heart of man than those who cloister to the city for whatever reason. Now, the herd animals' instinct is to continuously make everyone a part of the herd for there is safety in numbers. Also it means that their truth is *the* truth. That is not how it is. Learn to be a sovereign. Sovereignness is loving

55

yourself first, then letting the world do
whatever it wishes to and never judging it for
whatever action it does. So be it.

You have learned? You will. I will demonstrate
to you in the days to come in your time what
I'm referring to. Then you shall experience it
and you shall never forget it, it will become
wisdom upon your Soul. Desire you anything
else, Master?

MASTER Not really. No, that's enough. Thank you.
That's a big help; learning not to judge, that's a
big help. I'm learning not to judge so much
because those experiences are always there and
it's sort of always throwing up a guard toward
those things as a protection, really.

RAMTHA Judging is nothing to do with it. It is called
wisdom through experience. No one has to utter
one word—when the feeling occurs within your
Soul, the Soul [has] picked up the intent, the
intent is felt within the Soul as a feeling. Go by
your feelings, that is the God within you
speaking. He does not speak with a tongue, he
speaks with emotion. Go by that which is
termed your feelings. And when an entity
enters into your being and you have the same
feeling, know that that is your own well-earned
wisdom working for you. That is a blessing.
Love them and walk away from them. That is
not judgment; that is knowingness, Entity.

Judging others is to assume and judge them for
the way they are and the way that they live and
the way that they express. That, no man has
the right to do for everyone is expressing *his*
truth. Let your feelings and emotions guide

you; it will keep you blameless, Entity, and keep you into that which is termed noble virtue. So be it. Contemplate this. You will find it a great evenness.

Seemingly You Are Getting Nowhere But Really You Are Getting Everywhere

RAMTHA Master. Wondrous entity.

MASTER It almost seems that every question that I had has been answered.

RAMTHA It has been except for one.

MASTER I would like to be able to stop the inner turmoil. I seem to be able to . . . I know that I can manifest anything that I want to manifest in my life except that I seem to be able to manifest the negative much more easily, almost like in a twinkling of an eye and it's there in my life and I've got to deal with it. I'd like to make more of the purposeful good come about in my life, 'cause I'd like to feel happy about it. I'd like to do the kind of work I'd like to do. I like making films. I want to do that; it makes me happy. But I want to stop the internal battle—the "No I can't," "Yes I can," "No I can't," "Yes I can," "You can't," "You'll never," "Yes I will,"—I want to stop that inside.

RAMTHA The greatest conquest is the conquest of one's Self always. First off, Master, what makes you think that there is a negative at large?

MASTER I'm not sure I understand, *a negative at large.*

RAMTHA Well, you see, the purpose for good is continuously happening around you for a reason—for you to understand, to see, to be a participant in. If you change your attitude only for seven days in your time, Entity—that everything you do will never be negative again; that everything that comes about will be purpose for good; that there is no such thing as either good or negative, that there only *is*—then, Master, you shall see results called genius. It is the judging and the weighing of one's own Self that does not permit him to express that which is termed his own happiness.

Cease having division, cease having alterednesses; cease it—there only *is*. All the things that have happened in your life, you have expected them to be that way, then you have called them negative; then you have warred with [that] fact within your being [by asking yourself], *Can [I] really do anything?*

If you change your attitude, Master, for seven days—and this I will help you with—and see everything as *purpose for Isness* and remove that which is termed negative, failure, *cannot*, *can't* from that which is termed your knowingness and permit *is* and *Blessed Be I* for seven days in your time, you will understand what a change in attitude does for the wonderment of your being. The wrestling is that you are wrestling for a priority whether it is good or bad, or *you can* or *you can't*. You simply *are*. Can or can't, as it were indeed, is conjecturous after that point. The fact that you *are* permits you to be anything that you wish to be.

Your First Production

Now, you want to do that which is termed films? You will. Your greatest productions will not come until that which is termed the closing of the winter of this year that is already upon your calendar of understanding—your greatest opportunity. But until that point, Entity, everything shall be a learning concept that will open that which is termed the doors to the wonderment of experiencing Self. And your first production is going to be a production on the reflectiveness of yourself seen in the enactment of another.

And all that you shall learn between this time and that which is to arrive in your illusionary understanding shall teach you to be the great master that you already are. That is a certainty. Whether you can or you can't does not matter any longer, Entity. You already are that sovereign that is already into motion now. There is no such thing as negativity. There is no such thing as evil unless you permit it and create it and accept it that way. Evil, as it were indeed, is the acceptance of one overthrowing another. When you do not recognize it, Master, and know that your greatness is eminent, it never occurs and there is no such thing as evil. That is [what] the entity has to deal with in their own being.

It's In The "Can"

You *can* everything you want to do. *Know* that you can. Is; Am; imminent. I will tell you another thing for you to know. How is your destiny created? How is anyone's destiny created if everyone here be that which is termed sovereign of a god that is uniquely within them and they are expressing their truth? Who controls the destiny of that truth?

MASTER Each person.

RAMTHA Correct. How do they do that? What causes the tomorrow to come?

MASTER Desire.

RAMTHA Desire? What caused the events in that tomorrow to be evident in that desire?

MASTER I'm not sure I know.

RAMTHA Most don't for they do not see life in a simplistic view; they see it in a complexity. God is the simplicity of all things. Your very thought that you are having this moment, Entity, is being born into that which is termed feelings immersed into a light field within your entire embodiment, is recorded in your Soul and then becomes mass. The mass is the days to come.

Everything You Feel Will Come To Pass

Everything you are thinking this day you will feel, and everything that you feel will come to pass. That is orderly destiny that is occurring in this now. There is no future and there is no past. There is only this reckoning point called *now*. Everything else is wisdom. The Thoughts that you have—failure of Self, the lacking of Self-love—words, every word that you speak manifests! They don't even know it. They are looking for someone else to blame their failures upon. No! You are *God*. Remember that. Everything you think *is*. Every word that you speak is an open command in the source to *Be*.

The Father who loves you is judgeless and egoless. That which you speak, be it blasphemous to your own Self and negative, he thinks not as negative. Thus, whatever you think you are you will become, and he holds you in perfection always. That is the allowance of life to be in the next moment. But God, the Father, is the ugliest of all things and yet the heights of beauty and perfection and Isness for, to Him, there is nothing but Him—the degrees are seen through altered consciousness. Thus, if you conceive yourself to be negative, He will see assuredly that that shall become apparent in your life because you have ordained it. Your very words speak a command; every word that is uttered. Seemingly you are getting nowhere but really you are getting everywhere for you are getting exactly what you think you deserve and [you are] speaking it.

If It Works For The Negative, It Shall Work For The Isness

Now, in seven days contemplate the *love* of God; how great this Entity-Self is, that is all encompassing, that will allow you to be and do anything you wish and hold you judgeless. God has never judged you or anyone. If He has then He has judged Himself, for who be *you* but He. He has never judged you, so contemplate that His love for you is such that every thought manifests and every word manifests, and through that He has built your kingdom for you—*you* have designed it. When you infinitely also realize the splendid moment that be you God, that if you accelerated the thought into

Isness, into opulence, into all-consuming, into brilliance, into all-knowingness, that it would also be. For if it works for the negative it shall work for the Isness.

And if you change your words from Self-doubt, Self-damnation, and Self-hate into Self-*love*, into *is*, and cease asking the opinions of everyone else, you will find your fortunes and your knowingness will accelerate with great vigor. You are simply taking the law that you yourself created and bringing it into that which is termed the purpose for good by designing what *you* want. All you have to do is think it and feel it into emotion; then it is set, it will come to pass. That is how it is in this wondrous kingdom that you live in but have been ignorant of.

God Has Never Judged You Or Anyone

Seven days contemplate *you* and this wondrous God and all that you wish to have and love yourself for it. You will see wondrous changes as a result of it. So *be* it.

RAMTHA Rumps are sore, bellies are aching, and minds are full. Go and fill your bellies, and rest your rumps and minds. Do return in two hours in your counting for more.

DINNER-BREAK CONVERSATIONS

DISCUSSING THE OUTRAGEOUS ENIGMA

W I N D   B E A R I N G S

Self Central Station

DOUGLAS: Here I am with Miss X. So, tell me everything you know, Miss X.

MISS X: Do you have about five minutes? What would you like me to speak about?

DOUGLAS: Your first Dialogue. Can you give me a picture of that? From all points of view; from your hearing about it, from your arrival, your first impressions.

MISS X: Do you know how I heard about this? Okay, I'll take it from one step before that. I had signed up as a person whose work was in health and healing and things of that nature. I had registered for a course in healing with a prominent gentleman in the field. He is a man who does mind-to-mind healing and he had come up to New York from South Carolina.

I attended his class and beside me, unbeknownst to me, were a number of people who would become the first Atlantic City, New Jersey masters and the first New York masters. At the end of the healing course he shared with us an amazing experience he had during a reading in Seattle by a woman he had never met whom he subsequently did meet. A message had come forth for him and he had gone there and had met with her and he said it was the greatest thing that had ever happened to him in his life because he knew it was truth from spirit.

He played us this tape of this person named Ramtha who addressed him as Beloved Brother, Master, etc., called him the Torch Bearer because he was bringing light to these people. When I heard this tape I knew I had to have this experience, and so did a few others who were present at the healing meeting. From that encounter, Dialogues began to be established in New Jersey. My first experience was in

Atlantic City. Shortly after the Atlantic City Dialogue, one of the masters began to organize dialogues in New York.

I believe it was in April or May of 1979—the first Dialogue in Atlantic City, in one of the masters' living room. A group of very expectant people had gathered; apparently some had come from quite a distance. Everyone sat in a circle in chairs. The home was just a normal home in a quiet residential section. They made certain that it was quiet there. They had set up comfortable chairs all around the room. There were probably fifteen people present. There was a total air of expectancy as everyone sat there waiting for this person to walk down the stairs because no one knew quite what to expect.

We were there a little while and everyone was just totally silent, thinking—no one knew how it was going to start—when I looked up and saw this blond-haired woman coming down the stairs. She was very shy. You sensed a feeling of insecurity about her as she took her seat. She was wearing a pair of jeans and a little plaid blouse, quite fashionable at that time, sandals; she was just the normal woman, housewife, coming over to do her thing. She spoke a little to people beforehand but very little, very little. At that time she wasn't really speaking about J.Z. and her becomingness; her whole trip was Ramtha, not J.Z., because she was in the beginning stages herself.

We saw her, we experienced her going into her altered state. She said she would just sit there, and she told us to bless ourselves and to bless her, that it would look like she was going to sleep. Then her whole body would change its position and it would be obvious someone else was there. And it was! Ramtha's voice came through. The utilization of J.Z.'s voice then was different; it was not as fluid as it is now. He didn't move the way he does now; it was a stiffer kind of presentation, and the language was a little bit more archaic as he was getting used to, I assume, speaking, translating those feelings into words.

What is striking about that meeting compared to this very present meeting now is that Ramtha was saying the exact same thing then. Whatever he said to all of us was still the same unlimited mode that we experience today. He is even in his expression. What is most striking to me is, what a long way I and others have come to understand that which he was saying at that time.

The moment Ramtha came through all I could do was just weep on and off through the entire dialogue—it was an incredibly emotional experience for me. There is something of that entity that touches the Soul and stirs something within each of us that is literally lying dormant until it becomes awakened. That first meeting for me was just revolutionary, not to mention the things he said to me. I knew my life at that point was changing just from what he said, and I didn't even understand everything he had said to me at that particular point.

All of this was just a very new thing for J.Z.; you can imagine. When the dialogue was over she would say, "What happened? How did it go? Was it okay? Was everybody happy?" She gave and received a lot of hugs and kisses and it was fine and she was fine—that was the place she was coming from. It was not a knowingness even inside of her, at that point, of that which she was bringing forth to other people. What's also very striking to me then, as now, is the sincerity of J.Z. bringing forth this enigma; as a person who is devoting her life to doing this kind of thing. It's just very moving to me, J.Z.'s dedication to this. It's coming from a very sincere place within her, from her love for this entity and for what he has to share with others.

From A Head Place To A Heart and Soul Place

DOUGLAS: Since 1979 this enigma has been encircling your life. What have you derived from it?

MISS X: Well, I regard my life as being pre-Ramtha and post-Ramtha. In the beginning I had some difficulty because I was studying with another teacher. I had been studying with this teacher for about eight years, at that point on a weekly basis. Part of my own process was separating away from this teacher. Ramtha's teachings were simply more unlimited and there was no way I really could continue to listen to limited teachings anymore. I guess there was a point of devotion in there to my teacher and maybe that made the shift difficult.

Ramtha's teachings do not speak of being devoted to anyone but Self. They teach not to think that anyone is in a hierarchy or in a higher order than you are. So, for myself, I think basically it's been a process of moving the information from a head point of view, of intellectually understanding what he is talking about, to a heart and a Soul place, that it *was* a living reality for me.

We can all understand the words that he is saying to us but to make them a reality in our life is a very different kind of thing. So, for me, it's been a gradual, sometimes more accelerated process, depending upon how much more I could take in in my own moment of moving from a more circumscribed, limited, societal viewpoint as a child of society—being a "good girl" all my life—to a different place. I think my value system has altered as to what matters and what's important to me. Although I've always said that certain things were important to me, it's quite clear that this teaching has really shifted over to a living reality in my own life.

The Only Way I Knew Myself Was When I Judged Myself

The ways in which I've identified myself in relationship to others and in relationship to society have shifted. I guess that means letting go of ways I have identified my Self. The only way I used to know myself was when I judged myself in comparison with others. I stood on the scale which compared myself to others through the different roles that I have played in my life. I have learned that I played those roles to feel gratification for myself, to feel good about myself.

I have played the role of girlfriend, healer, therapist, workshop leader, good daughter—things of that nature. Then my roles moved more to fame, fortune, success, whatever I had been groomed to think that was all about. Then I moved to a more simple situation apart from all of those things, apart from all of those people and all of those situations. I have reclaimed my Self apart from all of that back to beingness. My success is based now on, *how do I just feel about me?* That is how I feel gratification now.

So, it was a shift from a doingness frame of reference to a beingness frame of reference—identifying Self because *I am* as opposed to what I can do and who I can help. My frame of reference now is just myself for myself just because I'm the God that I am. I rejoice in that. Time has taken on a different frame for me as well; I'm not rushing towards anything, my moments have slowed down and not become greater, and there is more room in my moment which I've learned from Ramtha.

DOUGLAS: Well said, "more room in my moment."

MISS X: What was interesting, in the slowing down process which you can epitomize with my moving from Manhattan to living in a tent for three and a half months; in that slowing down what has really happened is that there has been an acceleration of other elements within my own Self. That's the paradox within me: in the letting go of what you think you have, you gain it all; you gain something else. It's a letting go of one thing but it's an unfoldment of yet something else, which has nothing to do with anything outside of Self at all.

I think that my inner reality has shifted; though I might "regress," or do the same kinds of things that I've done in my past, that which is in my being which is projected into those things is very different.

DOUGLAS: Please talk about that shift in reality. What does that mean?

MISS X: I can only say it in an example. For the rest of my life I will probably be working with people doing whatever I will do with them—helping, healing, facilitating—whatever it might be as an agent for change. That is how I regard myself; as a teacher, which seems to be very important to me. In the past, while I was working as a teacher, I was attached to that in a certain way. My inner reality in regard to that was, *I knew something.* My inner reality has changed in the sense that I am no longer enslaved to certain outer things that in some way defined me. If I continue my work, or if I don't continue my work, I still know who I am. I am not defined by that which I am doing.

DOUGLAS: Perhaps that's why attorneys look like attorneys and doctors look like doctors—that which they work at defines that which they are.

MISS X: Yes. I might always wear nice clothing, I may always look acceptable on the outside, yet the inner reality attached to that *acceptance* has altered. In the past my inner reality was that I wanted to look nice to impress someone, or maybe I wanted to wear certain clothing when I was doing my work because I thought that that's what a professional woman would be wearing to do that job. Now, I can still wear those same clothes but I can also not wear those clothes and it really wouldn't matter. My inner reality attached to the acceptance of wearing those clothes has changed. A professional woman would wear whatever that woman felt like when she woke up that morning. It really wouldn't matter.

I used to dress for this image I portrayed for myself; now I dress for my Self instead of that image. And so, in that sense, my inner reality has shifted. I might have just called my mother, and in the past I had always called my mother. But what that telephone call means to me now is very different than it did before. I no longer feel responsible towards my mother; I no longer am hooked into her in the ways I have been in the past; I'm quite clear that I am not enslaved to the role of the daughter to the mother who calls the mother. Now, I do call my mother but I'm very free even when I call her; I can call her or not call her and I don't feel guilty about it, and I don't feel like I *have* to call her. Though the action looks the same as it looked when I called my mother in the past, it's different. The inner reality has shifted; I can come or go or whatever.

What's happened with my Self is that I have become freer within my Self; I'm not as enslaved to certain roles or expectations in a role. It is wonderful not to be enslaved to the *I wants*. My inner reality has shifted because there is much more joy in my life. It's quite clear that the major learning from Ramtha for me has been the love of Self; just the *love* of Self if we would say it in just a few words, and that takes many different shapes and forms. It's been very hard for me to understand that I could really do something just for me apart from other people.

DOUGLAS: So your motivation has changed from others to Self?

MISS X: Yes. Now, I don't feel guilty if I do something for my Self. I feel like that's all right; that's all right because I've gotten the idea that this is my responsibility in this lifetime—we each can be a greater light to others just by taking care of Self from a cleaner space within our own beings, a less attached kind of space. So my inner reality has greatly shifted and it didn't happen in one minute; it really has been an ongoing process. And there were a lot of fears which I didn't even regard as fears.

We can't know certain things that Ramtha speaks about because it truly is the unknown for us. And there is a moment which is the leap of faith within our own beings that we literally are willing to let go of something to just see what it would be like. And Ramtha can send any words to us but until we literally make that step we will not have the Self-sense, the emotion that indicates what knowingness really is. It's not in the mind, it's just Self-central in our own beings.

DOUGLAS: Self-central? Is that like Grand Central Station?

MISS X: Yes, from Self-central is where all your journeys emanate. I've had to let go of many things to be able to become Self Central Station.

DOUGLAS: Please expand on the leap of faith you mentioned.

MISS X: Okay. See, for me, I did not perceive myself as being that unhappy. Ramtha said to me, "You function very well in this city [New York]. I see you and you can handle it very well. The issue is, you can live here but do you want the quality of your life to be this way? Are you aware that you have to armor your Self? Are you aware of the fact that you know you are gentle and you are loving and you are all those things but are you aware those things can't really come out too much in this type of environment? Be aware that you are making a choice, and there is a choice."

Ramtha speaks about options. I was not one of those people who was miserable and unhappy; I didn't even know there *were* other options. So it was a little harder for me, I had my little kingdom really set up there and it was really working for me on one level. Therefore, for me, the unknown was letting go of what I knew to work for something more qualitative and deeper. But I didn't quite even know what Ramtha was speaking about.

DOUGLAS: Why did you continue with it if you didn't know, if you couldn't know what Ramtha was speaking about? It seems like you touched it but didn't know what you touched.

MISS X: Because it felt so terrific, it felt so "truth." What he was speaking of to me was very familiar to me and was just the way it was. There was nothing odd or strange on a deep level about what he was speaking about. I guess for a while I didn't personalize it to make those steps for myself. It was intellectually stimulative in a way.

DOUGLAS: But there was a felt knowingness?

MISS X: Which was true just right from the beginning because it stimulated that cellular knowingness of the God that we are, that God that I am that was blocked from my conscious mind. From the beginning of creation that cellular knowingness was birthed and has remained. It is a very primal thing that Ramtha touches in people, that he touched in me and continues to touch in me.

I went through many stages in terms of who Ramtha was to me. In a certain sense when you ask me why I kept going, I had to keep going because Ramtha triggered off inside of me a reminder to me of who I really was. What was clear to me was that I wasn't living that; that was not my everyday reality. When I went to the Dialogues I was reminded of who I really was in a very deep, deep sense. For my whole life I guess you could say I've been a seeker—I've been a person who's really known there was something more but didn't quite know what that was and how quite to get there. And I've looked into whatever avenues that were available to me in my own frame.

When I met my Self through the help of Ramtha, I knew I had just reached the end of the line of looking. Whatever I

had been looking for throughout my whole life, the realization of all of that which I didn't even have words for, was
possible through me! And so, for me, it never entered my
mind to not go on. I never missed a Dialogue when it was in
New York. I now know, for me, that I can *know;* I now
know that I can be all that I can be. The all that I can be is
every thing, the all in all. To me, Ramtha is a great ideal
because I do have a sense that we can live as Ramtha is,
even here, on this earth. And, as I say, that touched
something very primitive inside of my Self.

I also now have a feeling . . . in certain moments I wonder
why I've ever had one word in my entire life, about
anything. In those certain moments I have a total sense of
well-being—a *total* sense of well-being and peace of mind.
The mundaneness of my existence and the little dinky
things that we harp on seem to fade and a more important
Self-sense of joy and peace and well-being seems to
pervade. That is the feeling that I am desirous of having all
of the time. I consistently feel that feeling at Ramtha's
gatherings; I feel so loving I'm almost always giggling and
smiling about my Self.

DOUGLAS: After four years and a couple of million
words . . .

MISS X: . . . what am I left with? It's so fascinating because
after a couple of million words you are left with just one
word—Self. That message he's said in a million different
ways but that message becomes clearer and clearer and
clearer. He says, "I speak a simple truth," but we are so
complicated in our thought processes that we can't even
absorb and understand the simplicity of what it is he is
speaking about.

In My Moment, Right Now, I Am Enough

For me it's been the process of "cutting away"—going for
that which brings me the joy of including more and more

into my kingdom. I feel good for me. I, more and more, am having a sense of my "okay-ness"—that I'm all right. And also knowing that I don't have to keep on looking out there all of the time, and directing myself to things *out there;* knowing in my moment, right now, I am enough and I'm perfect and I'm enough. The more that I realize that, the more the moments really are joyful and happy.

There is no need to prove anything—especially my Self-worth to other people—but to just let myself be. That's a simple expression but it takes quite a bit to realize what that's all about. I have a better grasp on that now than I have had before. I feel much more relaxed in my own Self, for my own Self. I'm far less judgmental of my Self also, and of other people, and of other things.

As I've Judged Myself Less, I've Judged Others Less

I find that I let other people be more even too. I've realized at this point that everyone really does have their own truth. Each individual is seeing things from his own individual, unique point of view and I don't need to have others have my point of view, and I don't have to have their point of view, and it's okay to see things from whatever way you see them. It's been a process of allowing myself to want to find out what my point of view was apart from all other people, and then to, more and more, allow other people to have their own space without judging them. That has evolved from allowing myself to have more—allowing myself to have whatever feelings I am having in my working through of whatever I am working through.

As I've judged myself less, I've judged others less. Ramtha does not judge people. It is my great desire to move into that space—the unconditional love space without the need to define the word, *unconditional.* That must come for my Self first. I've grown to love my Self more.

DOUGLAS: How would you summarize it, then, in three words?

MISS X: What does it refer back to? Well, how would I summarize it? The running thing that Ramtha is trying to have us all get is: You Are God, I Am God. Yet, more meaningful than the words, it's a growing into the knowingness of that and what all that means, the infiniteness of that. All these categories we've discussed are a part of that: the love of Self, the lack of judgment, and the love and all that.

DOUGLAS: So you walk with a different gait now: you *know* you're a God, yet you don't have to stand on the street corner shouting it out.

MISS X: Yes, I've gained a much greater acceptance of me and other people and where we are coming from. But I can allow the other people to stand on the street corner and do whatever they are doing. Yet, if people are experiencing unhappiness I certainly will share with them some of the things that have worked for me, if they ask me to. There are a lot of reasons why we hold onto our beliefs to help give us an identity. It is mainly those things that are keeping us from our greater happiness.

DOUGLAS: What is the entity Ramtha?

MISS X: You asked me that yesterday. To me, Ramtha is a spirit like we all are, an entity like we all are, except he is not in the body. He is, simply, in knowingness of who he is *completely.* I really don't feel an apparent separation between Ramtha and myself. I just feel he is in greater knowingness of certain things than I am right now. He is a spark of the divine just like we all are—he is known as Ramtha and I happen to be known as Miss X. Ramtha is what he is calling himself; he's just an entity the way we all are.

DOUGLAS: Could you help to define the scope, the reach, the dimensions that he is able to traverse knowingly.

MISS X: I think that he is able to tune into the *total* river of thought of the All-In-All, and I think that allows him to be unlimited. We're limited to the extent that we can only tune into certain numbers of thoughts and thought patterns, so to speak, that continually are the parameters of our reality. Until we break loose and suddenly we see a new way of doing something or thinking about something, which is an "Ah Ha! Oh! Hmmmmmm . . ." that is growth for us. As far as I see it, Ramtha is not obstructed, he is not constricted by limited thinking; he has access into unlimited thinking. And so, at any moment he is not constricted by anything.

Ramtha is just a profound experience. The Ramtha experience is a profound experience. I feel that Ramtha is quite an amazing and loving individual. And the masters that are growing out of the Ramtha experience are bringing forth new understandings for this planet to consider within the conceptions of love and power, and compassion and humility.

DOUGLAS: My sincere appreciation. It was nice.

MISS X: It was lovely, indeed.

Where Are The Cheer Leaders?

MASTER: The choice to be around Ramtha and the choice to be involved in what he's teaching, in great part I believe, comes out of his ability to communicate an equalness and to reject the concept of the teacher/student hierarchy, as it were. In my past my focus has become, not the experience of my Self as God, not even my experience of being whole, but an experience of how to serve, which, in our culture, takes on an exceptionally altruistic and moral virtue, possibly because of the belief that our culture is very selfish—an egotistical, self-centered culture. In consequence, I have so often fallen into being a server instead of just *being*.

Those of us in our late thirties and early forties have just come out of the previous generations' various ways of being. They believed in the ideal of service, particularly via a religion. It has been only recently accepted that there could be other forms of worship; i.e., a guru or a teacher of great renown who one believes has certain spiritual qualities. It is very easy for us to fall into line and to follow. Perhaps we think all those followers can't be wrong. And isn't that how we think about the major religions of the land?

In my own experience it's not that I haven't appreciated some of the things that I've learned, but I realize now how incredibly limiting it was; how it kept me in a certain position, in a certain place that never fully allowed me to appreciate the totality of my own being. And, subsequently, I have a much greater appreciation of Ramtha's communication of that fellowship/followship mode of beingness. And at the same time, that greater understanding did not come without some degree of trepidation in the application of the full experience of what *mastership* means in my life.

We were talking about this last night, there are no examples around. Therefore, the understanding of how to apply the truth of what Ramtha is saying, within an environment and a culture that not only doesn't appear to be conducive to that but in some ways is almost hostile to that, generates a fear within me. That striving generates for me a sense of the concern of some of the very basic fears which are alienation; being out there alone, literally going for the full experience of being God, being whole, being complete without an organization around you, without your flag bearers, your *yay* people—"Yay . . . look, here comes a God striver, yay"—those to cheer you on to your Godness.

I'm A God? What Could That Mean?

Something that I'm working with right now—what is the meaning of *being*. What is the meaning of simply living in the experience of being God; how does that relate to feeding yourself, sheltering yourself, going to a movie—how does that relate to that? Prior to the Ram, I thought that might mean stilling myself, still and quiet. Well, now I'm told that Godness does in fact involve *living!* How then, is that done without pursuing, without living in a survival kind of way, or in a compromising way that involves yourself in labors, or acts that are not fully and completely in line with what you absolutely want to do but includes some degree of what you *have* to do? That, at this point, is a question that I am posing to myself.

And yet, at the same time, I think, even beyond all of that, for me, the greater opportunity is the experience of a peace of mind. Therefore, living to survive doesn't even become a concern or an issue, it may become a means of understanding its full application. But the rub there comes if I make the understanding of those questions a problem or a fear as opposed to, beyond all else, simply establishing a peace of mind.

So whatever step I take or whatever direction, there is a serenity about it, there is a peace about what I am doing. And as the Ram would say, "Not even a faith, not even a belief, but a knowingness," a full and complete knowingness which is actually a redundant way of saying it; if it's *knowingness,* then it is full and it *is* complete. Those are some of the things that I appreciate about the Ram. His teachings almost force me into my own kingdom of Thought.

Like The Plucking Of A Cord

DOUGLAS: Why do you listen to the Ram?

MASTER: It's interesting because the question almost suggests a conscious effort—why do I listen, almost like, why do I move from this spot to that spot. In fact, in some ways its a . . . I'm not listening; I am *listened.* The reason I say *listened* is, when the Ram speaks, or when I hear the Ram, or when I read the Ram, there's something within me that resonates a truth. So *listening,* the verb, suggests almost effort. And while what the Ram has to say comes in and I filter it through and I involve myself in the understanding and application of its meaning—as he would say, into emotion or feeling—at the same time there is no effort in really going to the Dialogue or listening to a tape because it resonates.

In that process of resonating within my being, I have become *listened.* I have become the noun from the verb. It's soothing perhaps; perhaps its not unlike, "Why does a fish swim in water," or "Why does a bird fly in the air, why does a tree grow in the soil, why do I listen to the Ram?" Because he's there, because he's speaking, because I'm listening. Hillary was asked why he climbed Everest. Because it was there.

DOUGLAS: How does Ramtha's energy feel on your being?

MASTER: It resonates. Resonates is a term that really encompasses the feeling of it because it is like the plucking of a cord that resonates or moves at a frequency that is in total harmony. The concept of resonance: the term images a frequency, a vibration, the plucking of a musical string that moves again at a frequency that is totally in harmony with my Self; where there is no effort. That's why I say, *I am Listened.* It's more of a state of being—there's the "ing" again. It's almost not active. It's a state of *be.*

Speaking The Unspoken

MASTER: Ramtha speaks the unspoken to people like it's an everyday occurrence; he speaks the "secrets" other teachers I have known have not spoken about. It's really never been mentioned through the years of my studies—the idea of realizing the totality of who we are. He makes it an accessible kind of commodity that is just, "Oh, yeah, you can be that way; why not!?" Everyone can be that way, everyone can be that special.

And he speaks of happiness and joy, of the happiness in joy, the happiness of joy that we can all experience all of the time by creating that if we so choose. Whereas most other teachings speak in terms of suffering and hardship, deprivation, long years, Ramtha says you can begin to live in a moment. Your capacity to embrace these new ideas, to let go of what has encumbered you, to be what you are, can be lived in the next moment. You don't have to study for ten years before you're ready for the "initiation." You are going to embrace these new ideals in a moment. Initiation has already been initiated; enlightenment is only a thought away. It can take a moment or it can take lifetimes. It's really up to you, but nobody can take the moment away from you. Enlightenment is only a moment away.

DOUGLAS: You were talking about, when does Ramtha connect with you as a counselor?

MASTER: Sometimes it's that instant and sometimes it's a year later. That suggests the scope of Ramtha. To me Ramtha is an entity like myself and everyone here except he is not encumbered by a physical body. He has also realized his own unlimited nature and the truth of the saying, *I and the Father are one.* Knowing he is a perfect reflection of the Father he feels that all kingdoms are within his own dominion, and he is able to manifest on any level in any way that he chooses at any time because he doesn't subscribe to the idea of limitation; he is at onement with all things, with all the elements. He is a totally manifesting and manifested God. That's how I think of him for himself.

And he, in his enlightenment program with us, is to teach us in whatever way he can to realize ourselves in the way that he has for himself. Because he says he is at peace at all times, he is happy at all times, he is blessed at all times, he can have anything he desires at any moment, and that there are joys beyond that which we can't even fathom yet that are a part of his everyday reality. He is infinitely loving and compassionate because of his complete acceptance of his Self, of who he is. Because he has complete knowingness of who he is, he is able to see who we really are without getting involved in our ego personality manifestations.

Ramtha has been so steadfast and even about the simple truth about who I really am. He is the only person I know who's actively spoken to me and other people about the God within and the possibility that that can be lived as an actual *living* truth within our lives. And to hear that we can bring that living truth of the God within into *this* life, that we don't have to go through a hundred more incarnations, is truly exciting.

These truths he has offered to everyone, not just a special select few who believe in a certain way, for all because that is their birthright. Liberation is everyone's birthright. He has offered to those of us who are stuck the liberation of unstuckness.

The Soul Responds To The Tremblings

The truth presented by Ramtha has allowed me to accelerate the truth within my being. He evokes the feelings of the tenderness of the Soul. He speaks to us in such a way which bypasses our altered ego. In so doing he acts as a catalyst element for change in our being because the Soul begins to respond to the tremblings within our own being, of its own awakening. After that happens, although he will leave the Dialogue, it has become *us* in what goes on. It is no longer Ramtha but he has stimulated us through the process of the "fire"; he awakens that. So it continues to happen within our own Selves.

That is the shining light that experiences; it is you, it is everyone present, no matter what their station in life, no matter what their upbringing has been, no matter what color skin, no matter who they are or what they've experienced within the moment. It is a reconnection, of sorts, to what we are. And that reconnection can become an earth-bound reality because no one is "too this or too that," or "not enough of this," to allow that to happen. Everything can be realized and changed with the desire to reconnect with the divine part of our Self.

YOU HAVE
LIVED
13,342½ TIMES

SHOOTING THE STARS

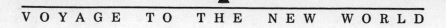

This Place Is The Emerald Of Your Universe

RAMTHA Alas, you have rested your rumps, aye?

AUDIENCE [Responds in laughter]

RAMTHA For those that are gathered here and come from that which is termed far places, I am pleased that you had the courage to leave your familiar surroundings and go out a little bit into the world. It is a very beauteous place. Everyone thinks that this place is called hell. Know what a *hell* is? It is an open grave, a shallow grave, to where an entity would be put because they could not afford the drachma or the rubies to be entombed, and because it was an open grave the hyenas and wild dogs took their feed upon the embodiments. That is all it ever meant until a later translation.

There is no such place as hell. There never was and there shan't ever be. It was a dreadful thing to create, to intimidate by fear and coerce the masses into a controllable organization. God, The Father, is much too much loving of your being and *is* all matter—every little grain in the sea, every little butterfly in spring, every vast star in the heavens, He is everything—and for Him to have had such a place would have been like a cancer in His body and it would have eaten Him up. There isn't [such a place]. And there is no devil, Lucifer, as he is termed. The entity [who] was called a Lucifer, was far from the entity you have learned him to be. There is only God.

And for this place to be called *a hellish place* is most unfair because it is the emerald of your universe. There is a planet that is affixing itself to become an orbital situation as this your planet we call Terra. It is called Venus in your understanding; it is very thick with cloud layer. Once your plane used to look the very same way; it is all of the oceans in the stratum that one day will be on the planet. That is

87

how the life forms that are living there wish it to be. But at the present there is none in this universe [as beautiful as your Terra. Even] though all inhabit life [containing] much intelligence, *this* is the emerald, for when you look at it from a distance the hue is bluish-green—it is beautiful. And so, for many in other places, this is called *heaven*.

Now, the world is not in the marketplaces, my beloved brotheren. It teems there with life [yet] the greater life is to be found outside of the marketplace on top of a snowy mountain, indeed, where the wind is crisp and cold and clean; or at the base of a magnificent tree that always intimidated soldiers, for though they were brave and strong not one of them was as grand as the tree who had lived for eons before their spoils came upon the plane; or looking into a brook and putting your feet in it and being one with the fishes. There is so much more to this your plane.

This is the *emerald* of the universe. Go to all of these places. Be a part of them. Put down that which is termed your silks and your jewels and take your shoes off. Be cluttered with unfashionable simpleness and go and experience God and this your heaven that you created. It is worth living for, it is worth being here for. I beseech you to do that, for you shan't have lived until you have lived in these places and been a part of their ongoing, forever consciousness.

I am called Ramtha, The Enlightened One, by my peoples and so I have kept that name even until this hour. An *enlightened* one? I was a solitary entity that sat on a plateau while everyone else did all of the things that they do in their daily days. And through this alienation of myself in the wilderness I found the Unknown God. And into those kingdoms have I tread and unto the promise have I returned. But you have not lived until you have become solitary in such a wilderness and at peace with the midnight sky and the moon that waxes and wanes until the brilliance of dawn—all you ever dreamed for—and in all the dreams and the knowledge that comes to you, behold you too will become the enlightened one.

Your priorities change there. The marvelousness of this consciousness of the wilderness accepts you, beloved brotheren. It accepts you; it expects you to be timeless like it is and in such circumstances can you grow boldly to become this God and to become steadfast in all the days of your life that are to come. I desire for you to do this. The Unknown God is silence—great silence. And yet, it will speak to you if you allow it to do so.

Just Know That You Are Ageless

RAMTHA   Desire you anything, Entity?

MASTER   Just to have all the fears come up.

RAMTHA   So be it. We do that straightaway. I ask you this for you to reason, God—what is the most fearing thing of all fears?

MASTER   Dying.

RAMTHA   Of course, but why is it that way?

MASTER   It feels like the end, not knowing that there is . . . it feels like the end of life.

RAMTHA   Dying is the ultimate fear of mankind. They live like there is not tomorrow for they are feared of old age and the worm. That is because they do not know how to live nor do they understand that which is doing the living. The ultimate of all fears is death. That is a truth, Master. Do you know you never have to die?

MASTER   I know that now.

RAMTHA   You never have to. Your body was made to live
forever; that the God that exists within it, that
it's image is Pure Light Principle that could live
into the eons of eternity. Your body was made
not to perish, Entity, it was made to express
through. It is only an instrument. Now, when
you know—infinitely—that you never have to
die, then what is there to fear after that?

MASTER   Nothing to fear after that. Just knowing that
you're ageless, that's the problem.

RAMTHA   Of course, but you will never know that if you
buy funeral plots and life insurance. What hath
God created that is grander than Himself?

MASTER   Nothing.

RAMTHA   Thus He has not created anything greater than
Himself. Then God is pure life and pure
thought. Then there exists no death within His
being, correct?

MASTER   Correct.

RAMTHA   You have nothing to fear. You have lived,
Entity, 13,342 and one-half times. You have
been every race of peoples existing from this
universe to the twenty-third to the seventeenth
to the one hundredth universe. You have
brothers, Entity, in your Pleiades, a most divine
constellation. You are a divine creature. Your
knowingness was absolute when you were a
babe. It has been limited to the point of
struggling to survive in this life without the
virtue of knowingness. And whenever you pass
this place you will pass, Master, in a twinkling
of an eye; you will be outside of your
embodiment, into the pure knowingness

principle of Light where you have come from and you will continue to live on and on and on. That is imminent.

I will manifest all of your fears to you, Entity, to the brink of death, and you will come back to this place and live for the reason you're suppose to be here—to *live*. Your destiny and everyone else's in this wondrous audience is to do nothing unless they want to do it—their destiny is to live. The reason they have come back here is not for karma or for judgment; it is to *live* and from that premise create whatever they wish to create.

You are going to learn to the brink of death, Entity, what life is and how precious it is. Then you will never fear anything ever again. And I will make you a light unto the world. So be it.

Go Out There And Live And Laugh And Judge No Man And Love All Things

RAMTHA   Master.

MASTER   Is there anything I can do in my life style at this time that will bring me closer to the grand Father and the Creative One?

RAMTHA   Would you do it if I told you?

MASTER   Good question.

RAMTHA   Indeed it is! Why would you ask me, Entity, if you would not contemplate doing it?

MASTER   I wouldn't have asked; you're right.

RAMTHA   That is correct. To bring you closer, simply this—you have never gone anywhere, you already are. All you have to do is know that and admit it to yourself. Closer means that you're far apart. You never have been; it never has been that way. Coming closer into the Father, Entity, into your Father, is simply *knowing* you already are. Everything that happens directly after that knowingness will only be proof and credence of the fact.

People think they must go through many things to get to those that they love. They do not have to. They have put themselves through it but it is not necessary. Wherever you want to be, *want* to be there. The reality will become blatantly clear to you. It's like in *God;* everyone wants someone that is bigger than them. Everyone wants someone that they can tell all of their troubles to and will continue to love them regardless. Well, there is such an entity. But the entity, Master, is not anything that you have to do—rigorous, ritualistic exercises to get to, nor to make laws to constrain yourself to be with—for no matter where you turn he will be there for he is the life of all things. When you recognize that he is closer to you than the hair on your head and the breath in your lungs, Master, then you know it is already imminent.

Simply love and enjoy this life and live it to its fullest capacity. That is loving God. All you have to do is know it. To change your attitude takes a moment, Entity: the moment is called *want.* Understand you?

MASTER   Yes.

RAMTHA   To some, Entity, this is much too simple; they must make it much more difficult and arduous and purge themselves and do all sorts of horrific things to themselves in order to be pure creatures of a loving God. Yuck! That is a limitation.

Go out there and live and laugh and judge no man and love all things. Find yourself in everyone you see. Hold yourself endearing and live this life, and cease looking at the bright signs in the marketplace and go out and watch a splendid sunrise or the moon—the enchantress will be out and you can see her wondrous beauty and see how everything turns magical. Look into the heavens—there are answers there, and movement. That is getting a little closer to this life and living it how it should be lived. So be it.

I will send you some runners, Entity, and if you look into the sky, a wonderment or two to help you. Go back to the understanding of what is simple, quiet and very much alive. So be it.

You Are A Wonderful Treasure You Have Not Seen

RAMTHA Master.

MASTER Ramtha, I'm happy to be here.

RAMTHA Indeed, I am pleased that you are here. You are a wondrous looking entity.

MASTER I would like you to guide me and show me how to improve the quality of my life, and I would like to have more drive and more ambition and find work that really brings me happiness. There seems to be a duality within me.

RAMTHA You're trying to make yourself do something you really don't want to do.

93

MASTER Well . . . yes, I don't think I really want to work, yet I do. I think it's expected of me; I'm fighting that.

RAMTHA Well, you see, work is one thing; happiness is another. You *can* be happy and be in a labor, but you're not happy at what you are doing. There is a wonderful entity who is elder in his age, as it were, that I send to you who will help you. The entity is quite a master though he would never admit it, and he will give you the wisdom without seeing you for the beautiful woman that you are, but seeing you for the God that needs understanding and will help you. We will open the doors to let you express. That will earn you that which is termed the gold which you need but also will bring you happiness. You're a wonderful treasure you have not seen. We do that in this your spring. So be it.

Drive and ambition—to be driven is not a proper way to live; you rush yourself to the grave. You should only be ambitious about that which you are, not about other people. That you need to learn.

MASTER This is a curiosity I have and think about often. I would like to know, is my father dead or alive, and is he or was he a good man?

RAMTHA He is alive. He is living in a place called France and the entity is a superb man . . . tissue for my Lady. Fatherns, as it were indeed, are born with the urge to impregnate the world and oftentimes some of them exceed. And there are those, Entity, that, because of love and circumstance, impregnate but do not always go about their own life feeling that all is well.

Oftentimes they are driven from what they
would like to be honorably doing. This is the
case of your beloved father.

Before this your decade is finished, Entity,
when this evenness has passed in your being, I
will see that you learn about your father. He is
a very good man but he was driven from that
which is termed his honor. Those who
impregnate the world lose count; he has not.
Now, I send you a wonderful entity who is elder
in age who is going to make your life wonderful.

MASTER I feel I already have that in my life.

RAMTHA Grander, Lass, grander. This is someone who
will love you, Master, in a greater
understanding than you have ever been loved
before, and will allow you to bloom better.
Change will be evident.

No One Ever Loves And Accepts Us As We Do Ourselves

MASTER I wish there would be more harmony in my
family. I have two families; my stepfather and
my mother.

RAMTHA Why do you wish this, Master?

MASTER To be with my mother more, to spend more
time with her.

RAMTHA So be it. I will arrange it. And what will you do
when you spend more time, as if it was of the
essence, with her?

MASTER We share wonderful feelings, thoughts. There is
a lot of quality in the times we share together.

RAMTHA So be it. We will arrange it to be a certainty. So be it. Desire you anything else?

MASTER I would like to know, am I loved by the people in my life; by the family members in my life now, the new family that I'm in, that I married into? Am I loved by them? Accepted and loved totally?

RAMTHA [A pause] No, not totally. Accepted indeed, but not loved for they have difficulty in discerning what that is as you will see. Why be that important to you?

MASTER I would like it to be that way, very much.

RAMTHA Why?

MASTER The need to be loved and accepted. It's very simple; don't we all have that need?

RAMTHA Ah, it is true, Entity, but unfortunately no one ever loves and accepts us as we do ourselves. That is the misconception. As long as you depend upon another to supply you with love and acceptance and keep you secure, you will have missed knowing what this life is all about, and you. You will only know what they want you to be. That is a subservient attitude that does not warrant sovereignness but warrants being a servant.

You, my lady, are worth loving and cherishing for you are the gentlest of creatures and beauteous, serpentine beauty. But Master, do not want everyone to be this way to you for you are wanting something that they do not have the capacity to fulfill. Then you will suffer the neurosis in your life of being rejected.

The importance is rather from a point of view of, can you love and accept them in their non-acceptance of you? How great is your love, aye? That is what is important here. Can you love them regardless of how they feel of you, aye? Can you indeed?

MASTER Can I in *deed*? I think I can. I would like to think I can.

RAMTHA My Master, I will show you that you can, and that is a victory within yourself. Then you are a great treasure that is very rare, especially in the cities where you live for there, Entity, there is nothing to do with the love of Self but [to live] some cloistered, imageless ideal of what everyone thinks you should live.

You'll become a treasure. Learn to love for the sake of loving, regardless if it is returned; that is exalting yourself. And where they grow old and wither, Master, you will stay young and fervent and will relish life. I will teach you these things in the days to come. Do not be dismayed. Look within yourself and love yourself for having the power to feel the way you do. So be it. 'Tis a grander way to live.

MASTER Thank you very much.

RAMTHA You are greatly loved, seen and unseen. Never you forget that. And one other thing, Lass. You belong to a whole; a whole that works perfectly within its own Self to rejuvenate life. You add to the quality of existence of all things. Know that, for that is a great truth. The love of God for you, Entity, there are no words for it. You are loved wholly for that which you are and what you appear to be. So be it.

The Whole Enchilada

RAMTHA Master.

MASTER Will the path for purposeful good be made apparent to me soon?

RAMTHA Know how?

MASTER No, I don't know. How?

RAMTHA Want! All you have to do is want it.

MASTER Well, if I want it and I have not yet felt that intuition, when I find myself going many directions, must I choose one direction?

RAMTHA Master, the path of purpose for good—who is the pathfinder?

MASTER I am.

RAMTHA So, if the path leads in many directions and you exhibit all of them, is that not purpose for good?

MASTER Yes.

RAMTHA The apparent knowingness of it, Master, is simply knowing that whatever you are doing is right. You have to be nothing other than what you are. Yet, what you are is everything that is. So you may venture and go any direction that you so please, Master, and wherever you go, Entity, you are going to be assailed with purpose for good; you cannot help it, you create it by your point of view of your direction. You may do and be and exhibit yourself however you wish. You have a grand spectrum in which to choose. It is all the right path. The right path is wherever you want to be upon it. That is indeed the right path.

MASTER But I find I lose my concentration.

RAMTHA What is concentration, Entity? Concentration
only denies you enjoying. I would much rather
have you have a jolly good time. If you have to
concentrate it is not worth learning.

MASTER Career-wise I find it's most important to
concentrate. But I find I enjoy myself much
more if I don't.

RAMTHA That is correct.

MASTER But then I find that that is sort of a paradox
also.

RAMTHA Then how do you cure that? Become the creator
of what you should concentrate on, then it will
come natural. You are a player, not a creator.
Whenever you play to anyone else's harmony
you are always going to have to memorize and
concentrate about what they want you to do. If
you were the creator you would not have to do
either; it simply would *be*. That is a much
grander way.

MASTER I wanted to do that.

RAMTHA So be it. We will allow you to do it.

MASTER I wanted the whole enchilada.

RAMTHA What was that?

MASTER I wanted the control over the entire project.

RAMTHA Oh, certainly. What does that equate?

MASTER Ah, knowing myself or my capabilities.

RAMTHA Ah, capability. You don't even have to
concentrate to have capability because that is
remnants of your own sovereignty. Wanting to

have control is merely wishing to express the creativity within you rather than following the rigorousness of someone else.

[There is a short pause]

What do you call this again? An enchilada? What be this creature?

MASTER   An enchilada. It's a Mexican dish. It's a food. It's a tortilla filled with cheese and meat and . . .

RAMTHA   . . . everything. Well, I would like for you to have the whole enchilada, Entity, in that which is termed your joy. You would have a great deal of joy in doing that and I will see that you do.

MASTER   Also, Ramtha, I have found this past year the physical body has taken a lot of trauma and I would like to know if that is all going to be alleviated soon?

RAMTHA   Do you want it to be alleviated?

MASTER   Oh, absolutely!

RAMTHA   Well then, love your body for how it is and let it express. That is keeping away the trauma. Love yourself; it will be an end of it. Your body is a most wonderful machine and it expresses perfectly; it expresses according to the commands of that which controls it. Love your body. It is a very good servant. The trauma will pass, Entity, and how you wish it to be it will become. But give it a little time to become that and really, I will leave you with this, Master, there is no such thing as trauma. That is a Self-ordained illusion. Everything is, really. I'm very pleased you have come to this audience. You have learned a great deal?

100

MASTER   Oh yes, not just from our discussion but from all of the discussions.

RAMTHA   There is a wiseness now. I send you a blessing. It will be in the form of flora. I consider them beauteous treasures. Keep them for a while, Entity, and make desires upon each of them. When the petals fall the desire will come to pass. So be it.

MASTER   Thank you!

RAMTHA   You are greatly loved.

You Contemplate Being Arrogant And Pompous!

RAMTHA   Indeed, what say you?

MASTER   I would like to learn or to have the strength and the will power to turn loose of relationships that cause me to have a lower amount of Self-esteem.

RAMTHA   Do you like having lower Self-esteem?

MASTER   No.

RAMTHA   Why?

MASTER   Because I think I deserve better but I'm not listening to myself.

RAMTHA   Well, if you think you deserve better and yet you do not listen, when you are ready to make up your mind to listen we will do something.

MASTER   Could the first step be coming here?

RAMTHA   Indeed. But Master, though that which is termed a wonderment that I be (and I certainly am), and all, as it were indeed, that flow from my being is a treasure, not everyone will see it

101

that way. Still they have their own will to
contend with and this I know. No matter what
I give you, you may do with it however you
choose to do with it. That is your choice. I give
unto you that which is termed the knowingness.
It is up to you whether you wish to accept it.
Keep it or do away with it, it is still given.

If you love yourself, wonderful Entity, which
you should, then you would love yourself
enough to deny yourself the pleasure of letting
anyone come into your life to demean you in
any fashion. That is arrogant and pompous and
that is how you should be. That is the answer.

MASTER   I thought that all the time. I want to thank you
most sincerely for bringing me here through a
loved one, and I want to thank you most
sincerely for those things that my loved one has
now. Thank you.

RAMTHA   Your loved one is most cherished by my heart.

MASTER   By mine too.

RAMTHA   Now, you contemplate being arrogant and
pompous!

MASTER   That's okay?

RAMTHA   Indeed it is!

MASTER   Okay!

RAMTHA   And you will draw to you someone that is
arrogant and pompous and who loves their Self
enough never to intermingle with another or
enslave another. Then you will have a wondrous
relationship, as you term it. Love yourself
enough to be not a part of anyone who wishes
ill-will upon your precious being. After all, it is

your being, your wonderful being, and it is time, as you would call it, to take stock of that being and live this life in a happy mode of existence with or without anyone else. I will help you.

MASTER   Thank you.

RAMTHA   Desire you more? Let us speak of your hovel.

MASTER   My what?

RAMTHA   Hovel.

MASTER   Oh, my laughing place.

RAMTHA   Indeed! Wish you to keep it?

MASTER   Yes, it could be a little bigger.

RAMTHA   I will see that it is made a little bigger.

MASTER   Thank you.

RAMTHA   And by all means do not sell it. So be it. I am pleased you have come here. And your beloved who has brought you, the entity has gone through much anguish and many teachers to try to find himself. But he will have to remember that Self is within Self. No one holds the key but them.

Only A Handful

RAMTHA   Master. Beautiful entity.

MASTER   My question, I guess, involves health, because at one time I was quite an athlete and I want this returned to me because it made me very happy for me, and when I'm happy with myself you give to others and I would like that.

RAMTHA   Well, when you are happy with yourself it simply flows from your being; it is hard not to be affected by it. So *be* it. We will help you to become that which is your desire and your dream, Entity. We will send you strength. It will become more prevalent upon that which is termed, as it were indeed, the becoming of spring. So be it.

MASTER   Thank you. Can I ask another question? I'm curious about my relationship with my oldest daughter. We have a bunch of pain from time to time. How could I get that under control?

RAMTHA   Leave her alone. There is nothing that brings greater joy and greater happiness to someone than it is to leave them alone and let them be what they wish to be.

MASTER   For better or for worse, right?

RAMTHA   Who is to say what is *worse?*

MASTER   True, can I ask another question?

RAMTHA   Indeed! Are you learning from the last?

MASTER   Your wit is quite great, I must say.

RAMTHA   Indeed it is.

MASTER   I'm curious if my book will be very successful in the months to come. I am collaborating with my sister.

RAMTHA   What do you term success, aye?

MASTER   Ah, a good definition of success. I guess it basically has to come through Self to do it; heavy publication throughout the U.S. and abroad.

RAMTHA   Why do you wish that?

MASTER   Because it makes me very happy to make other people happy by reading my stories.

RAMTHA And what if only a few do and they are very happy?

MASTER Well, I don't know. I hadn't thought of that. I hadn't thought of that in that way, but that would make me happy too.

RAMTHA Do you know that only a handful of people can change the consciousness of an entire world?

MASTER I'm finding that out.

RAMTHA Your books will be a success.

MASTER I have one more question. I'm curious, what was my last lifetime. What was I in my last lifetime, to help me more or less in this lifetime?

RAMTHA A sailor who sailed, as it were indeed, from that which is termed the port of Italy through that which is termed Crete, who had the greatest experience of its entire existences upon Crete. The entity found that which is termed a fledgling and the child became, you call them *warrant*. And the sailor took the child wherever he went and brought him to that which is termed a place called America and to a port that is to the far north. The child became a wondrous entity in law, went to school through that which is termed the help of the old mariner and became a change, as it were indeed, in the government procedures within your country. This was the only time you ever expressed as a man but still obtained a maternal instinct.

Your death, Entity—you died, as it were indeed, through that which is termed a fire, and the fire consumed that which is termed a holding house or a lodging house; [you were] put to the back quarters because it had a view of a particular oak tree and there the entity perished within that which is termed a fire. Contemplate it. You will find there is memory in it.

MASTER I saw quick flash-backs.

RAMTHA You skipped all these miserable wars that lay siege to the land, and that was very wise on your part. They never do anything. That was your last life and that was a good one. The child was a good one also. So be it.

It Has Been Rather Lovely

RAMTHA Master.

MASTER I wasn't expecting you to talk to me just now.

RAMTHA No one ever is.

MASTER I've always had dreams starting when I was very young. And these dreams—I've continued to have them through the years—always I can feel people; I can feel the emotions, what they feel, and what they're thinking . . . but I have a problem, no problem!

RAMTHA You have learned well!

[Laughter]

MASTER I would like to learn control of not being *how* they are feeling. I want to just feel what *I'm* feeling. But it seems like their emotions or what they feel is in fact what I feel. I would like to control feeling their feelings; and I want to get more involved in my piano playing. I believe that would be very good for me. I definitely would desire a soulmate. Yes, let's see here, I want a . . . [audience laughter] . . . let's see here,

I want . . . this is beautiful being here with you. It's great, it's a beautiful feeling.

RAMTHA   I am pleased that you have come forth and are having your desires; that pleases me greatly. But let me tell you this, Lass, feeling for other entities is a very rare thing. Most have turned themselves off from other entities, thus the lacking of world-love for one another. Would you not agree?

MASTER   I would agree.

RAMTHA   The reason that you feel the way that you do for others is that you have the capacity to *be* that which is termed the other. And through that, and only through that, can one gain true understanding and help other individuals in the face of it. What it will teach you, Master, is how to ascertain and reason from your feelings direct answers, helps, and cures for those entities, and it will work. Continue to feel that way—never get rid of it, that is a treasure.

From this day forth I bless your mouth, your wonderful Soul and your wondrous hands and your entire embodiment, and accelerate the feeling. And whatsoever you say, Entity, will come to pass. And however you give what is called advice unto another, the advice shall work and you will be called a prophet, a healer and a lover of mankind, and that is a great and wondrous thing. That, Entity, is grander than being chairman of any board—*that* is creating it.

You Have The Song In Your Soul

Now, in regards, as it were indeed, for that which is termed the piano, the piano is really a lopsided harp. If you will learn to sit down at

your wonderful instrument with nothing to
show you how to play, and contemplate the love
of any of these entities that you have felt so
intently for, and then think about them and let
your wondrous fingers begin to electrically find
the right note, you will find your music is
divinely inspired. And that, Entity, is worth
listening to and playing.

You will find you are a prodigy but in a greater
sense of the word. It takes emotion, great and
in-depth emotion to become an artist—a
musician as it were, a declarer as it were,
pretender—for the emotion allows the freedom
to express beyond the boundaries of limited
thought. That you are abundantly filled with.
Your emotion is wondrous. Allow yourself to
play and allow the harmony to come forth from
your soul and to fill the air with your sounds.
That will be a blessing and a healing to all who
listen to it. That I cannot do for you; only *you*
can do that for only you have the song in your
soul, not I.

Love—The Wild, Free-Moving Essence

Now, Soulmates—everyone has one. Most,
Entity, do not realize they do. They go through
their life having marriages and relationships on
top of relationships but they are really in
search. They are in search for *themselves* for
the Soulmate reflects that which is termed the
perfect Self back. Once you know you have such
a thing, that is what draws itself to you. That is
imminent. So be it. Indeed.

Love, it is a wild, free-moving essence that
edifies our beings, that glorifies our beings and

gives credence to our beings, that brings back
the youth in our beings; and if shared with
another, truly love, Entity, it is the deepest
intimate thing that any two humans can share
with one another, that exalts them beyond time
and space and measure and beyond judgmental
condemnations of others.

For eons in your time man has searched for this
wonderful feeling and yet, he has given over to
dogmatic beliefs, he has cloistered himself, he
has defamed himself in order not to have it but
in the name of searching for it. It simply *is*
when we become *simply,* and take that which
comes to us, that whatever face it wears, if love
(that feeling) is born within our being, it is
recognized of our being. Share the moments,
however long they be with one another. That is
a grand thing that one does with ones' Self.

Kingdoms have been fought, countries have
been lost, masses of people have been slain in
the name of it. What you are asking, Entity, I
am pleased, as it were indeed, to open the door
to release your being that you draw to you the
likeness of your being. Remember the feeling
and have it with your *Self.* Whatever you are
you will draw to you the equal of. I will see
they come to you. You continue to love your
Self, Entity. The feeling, it makes all things
worth all things. So be it.

MASTER Indeed! This is lovely.

RAMTHA Indeed it is.

MASTER Ah, there was something else. The dreams, the
dreams that I have. It's like an omen?

RAMTHA What is an omen?

MASTER Future tense?

RAMTHA Everything is future tense, Entity, everything. Even realization is future tense. Indeed, that is what they are.

MASTER My past life?

RAMTHA Forgotten.

MASTER Forgotten!? Oh, I see.

RAMTHA Like the moment we spoke earlier is past—it is now the past, it has just passed into the past. All that is bright and assuming in the realization is *now*.

MASTER Great! I would like to know, the position that I'm holding right now, is it time for me to make a move? Sometimes I feel like it's time to move on to another company or . . .

RAMTHA We will prepare a place for you to express your brilliance and your emotion. Be at peace where you are, Entity. The opening will occur. So be it. And it has been rather lovely.

MASTER It has, it has.

Eight Thousand Moments Of Now

RAMTHA Master.

MASTER First of all, may I ask how I can achieve perfect health?

RAMTHA What is perfect health? Is there such a thing?

MASTER I would think so, yes.

RAMTHA Tell me what it would be then?

MASTER Unobstructed energy, joy, great strength and the ability to do whatever you want to do through this perfect health.

RAMTHA That is all attitude, what you have just
mentioned. So what is perfect health?

MASTER Perfect machinery, I might suppose; body in
perfect condition.

RAMTHA It is whatever you conceive the attitude to be,
the machinery will follow. Unfortunately, no one
knows what perfect health is here because they
all die too soon to find out. Perfect health is the
abstinence of age, would you not agree?

MASTER Yes.

RAMTHA The attitude is what allows everything else to
work. Perfect health is dependent upon your
thinking, your body thus follows suit.

MASTER Well, then my will is weak.

RAMTHA Your will is weak? Your ignorance is weak. No
one knows, Entity, that they can sustain life far
beyond that which is termed, what is it in this
day, a hundred years that you can live? Do you
know that once they lived for thousands of
years and there are masters still here on your
plane that are eight thousand years old. Really,
it is not old, it is eight thousand moments of
now that they have expressed and they have
not gained any age.

Do you know how they did it? Your scientists
have them recorded and are studying them,
Entity. They never allowed the consciousness of
depleted-Self to occur, nor did they ever
regulate Self and condemn Self, nor did they
ever contemplate dying. That attitude allowed
the enzyme prevalent within their body and
allowed the hormone structure to be balanced.
They are still alive. Here everyone expects to

grow old and to perish. It is an awesome horrific thing to do to man. And for man, even greater to accept the concept. What if the concept was contemplated on the utopia of man rather than his doom?

MASTER That's how I feel.

RAMTHA You are going to learn how to express it, beautiful Entity. Never have another birthday celebration in celebration of your age. They are only celebrating your imminent death; that is not fidley. Start living *now* and always live *now*.

MASTER I have a headache right now, certainly. And since I've come to this country I seem to have more headaches. Would that be an attitude or the smog or the wrong foods?

RAMTHA Never the wrong foods. The headache is from the consciousness here. This is a very stressful consciousness, a very competitive one and ruthless. If you die they will only curse you that you are in their way. That causes anyone to have a head that aches. Leave the torrid consciousness behind, Entity, and seek you a place where the consciousness is more of the land. A tree, a great mountain, a desert, flora—they enhance that which is termed the human spirit; they never take away from it. Do a little bit more of your living here. And when you have to go into the city, bless the city and everyone in it. Then go and do your business and then leave it, it is a stagnating pond. So be it.

To Be The Last That You Want To Be

RAMTHA What say you, Lass?

MASTER I would like to learn to be less resistant to change; and to love.

RAMTHA   Would you like to learn to be less resistant to change?

MASTER   Yes.

RAMTHA   Then we will make the changes so that you can not resist them. So be it. That also answers love.

[Laughter]

MASTER   I was wondering from where I came?

RAMTHA   There is a cemetery in a place that is called—you have so many countries in this country—an Arizona. There is a place called *Bisbee;* used to be a wonderful metropolis there when silver was prevalent in the land—it was quite the place. There still is silver there and you are buried there and the name is *Martinson* and the beginning initial is *C* for Catherine. You perished of small pox, the dread of that which is termed the community. You go there; you will find your remains.

Who were you? A woman who had reached that which is termed the adolescent age of that which is called eighteen, had been married to that which is termed a wondrous carpenter at age fourteen, had already brought forth two sons and thus your lineage is still there. You can look them up in the records. And why have you chosen to be you? Because you wanted to, that is the answer.

MASTER   To do what?

RAMTHA   To live, that is the first desire of anyone who re-enters this plane, to express on what is called the Plane of Demonstration. Here you can

113

demonstrate any ideal and any attitude and it will formulate itself into a reality. But the true game here is not getting lost in it. That is the reason. You are not here to fulfill any prophesy or to fulfill any laws or to balance any karma—there is no such thing as karmic justice. You are here to live: to be the last that you want to be; to find the love of your life; to incorporate that love, most appropriately, in happiness. It is really a rather simple plane to find happiness if you only look. And if you look, Entity, the desire will take you there that you may be a part of that happiness.

Open up your eyes and look around you and never contemplate again getting rid of yourself or the unworthiness of yourself. You are a most beautiful entity. The love that you have within your being, that will always be there. You have not always had around you all the entities that you need to bring that to the surface, but you will. Be glad for it.

I am pleased you have come forth and this is a most wondrous color that you have upon your personage. If you were to put that on your wonderful carpets and walls, whenever you sit in such a room it would bring eminent peace. It is the first color that transcends the white light into gold. The only one actually. Very appropriate. [The color is violet.]

All That You Were Then Is Not As Grand As You Are Now

RAMTHA I would like to tell you this for all to understand. All have lived many lives. They have been illustrious, romantic, barbaric,

insidious, infamous, famous, no thing, some
things, part things, all things. They have been
every thing. But who is the greatest reflection
of all of those lives? Some will say when they
were a king was their greatest life. Obviously,
they had power over everyone else. Some will
say they were the most beautiful woman that
ever lived; that gives credence to find some
kind of pleasure within how they look now.
Some will be valorous and some will be fearful.

But I will tell you a truth. All that you were
then is not as grand as you are now. You are
the greatest you have ever been, Entity, for you
are the accumulated knowledge and experience
of all the things you have ever lived into this
now. What is that worth when you cannot be a
king or a queen? That is worth eternity, life,
God now seen. Collective wisdom is collective
experience that provokes us into the greatest
part of our genius, which is the mind of God,
and becoming him explicitly where there is no
doubt.

You have *never* been better than you are now,
no matter the disguise or the illusion or the
experience. If I was to de-vance you, Entity,
into five lives before, you would not even
recognize your Self, you would not even know
who you are. Even [in] your last experience you
would be a stranger for the intelligence you
possess now, the wisdom you possess now,
would be far superior to the entity that would
be you in a lesser lifetime. That is a truth.

Those who continuously look back into the past
to find out who they were then are never
finding a future and never even know the now,

for all of their yesterdays make up their nows. All of the same things make up the *nows,* which causes an entity [who looks back into the past] to be less creative, less prosperous, less loving of himself and insecure, for he gives no reason if he was so good then why he is now.

Learn to live in the *now;* the greatest life there is, the greatest being there is, the most beauty there is. Be *grand* in this life and experience you. Ride the wind, Entity, sail a thought to the moon, lay a splendid thought on the sun that it will know who you are, sit upon a star, speak to the water. That is all *you,* it is all God, it is all life, the greatest purposeful reality there is when all else is illusion. So be it.

Free The Soul To Fly

RAMTHA Master. What say you who hides behind this entity?

MASTER Hello, Ramtha. I'm glad to be here. I had so many questions for you but I've answered them all.

RAMTHA Are you pleased with the answers?

MASTER Yes.

RAMTHA Now, it is one thing to say, *I have the answers;* it is quite different to experience them. You have yet to experience them and that will be the great learning of this day. Master, you are a beauteous entity, never forget that. You live for these changes for they bring about happiness and they free the soul to fly, and to create, and to be whatever it wishes to be. Be happy.

MASTER I am, thank you. One more question, I would love to experience an astral flight.

RAMTHA So be it. Now, you will not be afraid?

MASTER I think that I will still go ahead and do it anyway.

RAMTHA Master, when you do this there is no fear and you will have it. It will come when you least expect it so you will not say that you dreamed it up. So be it. Be happy!

Give Up The Priority Of Being Unhappy

RAMTHA Indeed.

MASTER Several things. Well, first off, so far I've lived and it's been so great. If all I'm here to do is to live then it's just great!

RAMTHA But that is all you're here to do. You create the *must* and the *have to's* and the *can'ts* and the *failures*. But you can also re-create them.

MASTER Well, I feel like I should have some form of expression, some form in which I express myself more. You know, the talents I have, and teachings and things like that.

RAMTHA How would you have the form to be?

MASTER Some form of a retreat, like an ashram—something where I could work with a lot of different people, lots of people coming through.

RAMTHA Do you have all the answers?

MASTER No! I would probably be learning too

RAMTHA Indeed. Entity, what is difficult about that, that often those set themselves up to be the absolute. Then they forget what they are supposed to learn and thus all their teaching is very cloistered to only the point of view to which they've reckoned it to be. Then you have a following that depends on you for only you have the answers. That is not advisable, Entity. Do you know why it isn't? Tell me.

RAMTHA   Because it would be so stagnating. I would stop learning if I did that.

MASTER   Indeed. Then go out and live and forget about having a place to help people. In life, every moment—there are a whole group [of people] here that are interacting this very day—that by your presence and your word and your beauty you have taught them as well as they have taught you. In life, Master, the greatest learnings are for the valuable experiences that lie out there, not cloistered up in some stagnated, smelly place. You understand?

Now, we'll advance your knowingness. Be open and receptive to all of the things but ponder this one thing for me—what other reason would you be here other [than] to live, aye? So what does that all entail? Have you gone out and grasped a hold of it yet? Contemplate this—the things that you don't want to do you've already done. The Soul has already recorded all of the wisdom from those experiences. That means you have already done it. The things you have longing for, go and do them.

Let nothing bind you, Lass. Go and experience and be jolly glad you did, for in that are you learning of this wondrous place called Life and the joy and the happiness of being the eminent

God that you are. Then your inner actions and your way of expressing will help many others in their understanding. Just be—being is the highest and greatest treasure there is for that allows all the others to come to you. Do you understand?

MASTER Yes.

RAMTHA Let us go on with the next, aye?

MASTER I guess the next question was where I would be settling?

RAMTHA Anywhere you want to be.

MASTER All of the time?

RAMTHA All of the time. If I tell you one place, is that not stagnation? Where you want to be, Entity, *is* where you want to be. That is where you should be. If you go beyond that then you are denying yourself learning. Then you are becoming the stagnated teacher again. Go where you want to go and stay however you want to stay.

MASTER What should I do to maintain my health? The same things you said for others?

RAMTHA Give up limitation! Give up the priority of being unhappy, that is all you have to do. You are greatly loved, Lass. It will be a most wondrous time to come in your time. Be very fruitful for you. And when [there] comes a point in time to where you must do some measuring as to how you have advanced, you will be awed by how much you have learned. *Enjoy* this life. That is what it is here for. Love *everyone* who participates in it and let them be and leave them alone. So be it.

119

The Storm Will Cease

RAMTHA Master.

MASTER I have a little problem, I guess it's a big problem, of self-destruction. I seem to get into situations where I can't win and somehow it feeds me; and it's difficult but I keep taking that—getting into self-destructive situations. It prevents me from doing other things I want to do.

RAMTHA Tell me what you have contemplated when you have contemplated death?

MASTER Well, a lot of things, but I never really made it. But a lot [of] times I feel like I'm slipping away.

RAMTHA I understand that, Entity. Would you like to go?

MASTER Would I like to?

RAMTHA Would you like to leave this place?

MASTER No . . . not really.

RAMTHA Why do you want to stay here?

MASTER Well, I like to live. I think I'm here to live and it's difficult sometimes.

RAMTHA Who makes it difficult?

MASTER Well, I do.

RAMTHA Why?

MASTER I don't know.

RAMTHA My beautiful Master, you are a child of your society, a product of your family and their creed and heritage. That is very dismaying. If you were allowed to live, how would you live that would be an ideal for *you*?

MASTER More simple than I am living.

RAMTHA That is a correctness. I will do this for you,
Entity. I will remove the complexities and make
you a simple man, and I will send from your life
those who cling to you because of its
complexities. I will make you a simple man. No
matter what you do you will not destroy
yourself until you become simple. Then you are
going to live a little bit as a simpleton. Not
simple of mind or of intellect but simple in
harmony, Entity. And you will have a restraint
on yourself from making your life complex. I
will do it straightaway.

The storm will brew, Entity, and the thunder
will roll in the heavens, and it will roll in all of
those that are around you. Remain peaceful and
love yourself. Remain peaceful and love
yourself, Entity. When you've become simple
you will know it—the storm will cease.

Now, after you have lived this way, if this
makes you unhappy you will pass this plane
and you will go into a place where you will not
be coerced into being anything other than what
you want to be, and it will allow you time for
contemplative thought. There you shall
contemplate the priority of what is called
existence, the priority of what is called *Self*.
And when you have concluded that the priority
is nothing but to *be*, you will return to this
plane again and you will return a happy man—a
happy man. I will help you.

Your desire is sincere. You are a good and noble
creature within your being. You are here
because I desire you to be here. I've listened

and seen everything in your life and all that you have tried. It is time to recognize the quantities that exist there. We shall do that in the days to come. This will be a thundering process but it will be a slow one. Be at peace. I love you and that shall never cease. And I will help you to become that you can be a light unto others if they so choose to look. Indeed? Now, is it worth losing all the complexities for?

MASTER   I think so.

RAMTHA   You are worth living for, Entity. And to leave you with this—you will never really die, for escaping your body answers nothing. Desire you anything else?

MASTER   Yeah. I could be more giving to people I care for.

RAMTHA   Do not give to them, leave them alone. No matter how much you give it will never be enough for you have nothing to give except despair. You start giving to *you*. They will be the benefactors of that Self-indulged love. So be it. These are not mere words, Entity, they go greater beyond that—they will *all* manifest. We are going to see you into a place of simplicity where you can view things—the simple understanding. So be it.

This Picture I Have Of Me

RAMTHA   Master.

MASTER   I have created a couple of desires—obviously many—and a couple of desires have been repetitive through the years, that have carried on for a long time. I feel they have not

manifested or I'm still working with them, and
sometimes now it's like I feel like I want help in
making them be or being gone with them so I
can get on with life.

RAMTHA   Are they outside of that which is called the
perimeters of life, aye?

MASTER   No, not at all.

RAMTHA   So they are *getting on with life* also. Are they
not?

MASTER   Yes.

RAMTHA   What will you desire?

MASTER   One is in terms of my own health and vitality:
wanting to create a body that looks a certain
way; or be supple and free in movement, more
so than I think now perhaps I am.

RAMTHA   Why do you wish to be this way?

MASTER   Partly it's a picture I have; partly it's an idea I
have that I can create for myself, my reality.
Somewhere in my life I have created this
picture of perhaps what I want to look like or
be.

RAMTHA   You have and you are! You, Entity, created
you. Your parents, they added the fire but you
added the life and the design. You are exactly
how you wanted to be. Now, you wish to change
that?

MASTER   At times.

RAMTHA   But who has made you want to change that?

MASTER   Myself.

RAMTHA   Ah, but how would you know that you would

like to change it without the reflections of other critical eyes?

MASTER   Perhaps I wouldn't.

RAMTHA   If you would have never seen anyone else say, "This is how you should look and be," you would have been most content to be what you are and said, "This is how *you* should be." My Master, you can be anything you wish to be. But the important point and earnest issue here is that you are trying to escape your most beautiful Self. You know, what others possess, perhaps because their body is put together a bit different, they do not possess the things that you [possess] because your body is put together the way it is. The point is—you are unhappy with yourself but your body is not *yourself;* it is totality. *Yourself* is the attitude that you have toward you. Your image has been most unfortunately distorted to you.

If you want to be this way simply because it adds already to the beauty and the virtue that you possess, that is a wise decision and a good desire. But if you want to change it to appease the world so the world will accept you more because you look a certain way, that is a truth but it is in retardation. This world does not know what beauty looks like, for that is imageless and there is no ideal on this plane that represents the ideal in anyone's embodiment because they keep dying.

Your Image Should Be Yours

I find you beautiful and whole and earnest but with a great dislike of Self because of what you look like, how you appear. That we are going to

change, Entity, and we will do it in that which is termed the context of getting on with that which is termed living. You *earnestly* put [your Self] to it to prove this point to you. I'm going to arrange for that which is termed a wondrous encounter that will involve you and three others. You, Entity, will be the hero of the day, and for two for the rest of their lives, and you will see them trying to be like you. We are going to do this for you—you need this. Then you will help teach them to be themselves like I am doing with you.

You are a wondrous flame, Entity, that does not bear an image only to brilliant light. Wondrous, *wondrous* form—this body only serves as a vehicle of expression of that beautiful light. Love it, *love* it—it is precious. I will help you to see what I have just told you.

Now, For The Next Little Detour In Life, What Desire You?

MASTER I have for many years worked at being able to create a vehicle for expressing on, what I call, *a creative level*, particularly through music and voice and song. I have come close to that and far from it, and it feels sometimes like I'm struggling with it rather than just letting it be there. And I *know* that it's there—I've been there, I've felt it, I've been in touch with my creativity and yet, at times, I put myself into doubting it and stopping myself from just letting it be.

RAMTHA Did you enjoy doing that?

MASTER Right now it feels like, *No, I didn't enjoy that.*

RAMTHA   Master, you have not fathomed what a creative
entity you are because you doubt that which
you are already. When you cease doubting and
simply allow you to flow forth you will have
your perfect instrument of expression. Simply
permit *you* to be—leave you alone and do not
compare you to anyone, you will never find
anyone to compare to you. And by all means,
never ask anyone if what you are doing sounds
good, looks good, or is good. They will never tell
you the truth as you wish to hear it.

Get out of your way and allow you to be. And
that we allow, Entity, allowing you to see the
beauty of your own body and the beauty of
your own fine instrument that you are already.
Then, by leaving it alone and loving what you
are and not changing anything about you, you
will have all of your dreams come true. Most
entities, they fight their brilliance. They do
because they are always looking for an excuse
or someone to condone it. Leave yourself alone
and simply let it be, aye, and get on with this
living. You are a fine artisan. I have listened to
you. You are here for me to tell you to start
listening to you also. Then you will have the
answers to everything you wish to know. So be
it.

Making You Happy Must Already Be There

Now, you could run up and down the
mountains, Entity, and starve yourself into
oblivion and everything you wish to do. That
will not make you happy. Making you happy
must already be there. Then, doing all of these
other things are only extra things to allow
yourself to participate in for whatever end

result you wish. So be it. I am pleased you have come forth.

MASTER I am pleased to be here.

RAMTHA Am I any less of an entity because I appeared in a woman's embodiment?

MASTER Of course not!

RAMTHA Indeed. Am I any less of what I once was because I look small in stature now? Then do not be deceived by looks, Entity. What I am so be you. Contemplate that.

The Raising Of Mere Man Into Great God

RAMTHA Indeed, indeed, in deed; I am always offering that which is termed, *indeed.* It is in action, in truth, in essence, Isness, now, totality. *Indeed* is the affirmation of reality. What grander way [is there] to salute that which is termed Gods in the manner in which they should become accustomed to, than [by] acknowledging their reality? What, above all things indeed, does man retain throughout that which is termed the life—whether it be in misery, suffering, happiness? What does man always keep with him? His divinity. Man, God—the Divine.

You Are A God That Needs To Remember

Now, all that we have talked of this day, and not talked of this day, has been learning about that which is termed who be you. What be you? You *are* God! Man expressing as God often forgets that which is termed his Godhood, thus makes him grovel in the marketplace for survival. 'Tis not the way it is. You are a God that needs to remember. When you leave this audience you are no longer that which is termed mere man but you are that which is termed the Lord God of Your Totality, and you speak as a one rather than a duality.

And whatever you think will come to pass, whatever you speak will come to pass. You shall be director of a greater kingdom that you have never known before, all from the Lord God of Your Totality. Then who serve you indeed? And who love you indeed? Nay, there is no teacher save *you* the teacher. And who be your master indeed? There is no master save *you*, Master. And who love you? *You*. And you will learn to be kind and kindle the spirit of well-being for Self.

Then when you have learned to live as God lives, as God is—the One-ment with all things—and *behold*, you shall be a light unto the world, that by your being indeed, by that which is termed your Isness, that the world can see readily an ideal to which is attainable by all who but have to open their eyes and see. Now—mere man, no; mere God *indeed!* When you leave here you will go through "fire" for you will see things which you've never seen before. And there are those that will fall away from you that will love you not, for you have become *you* rather than them. There shall be those indeed that shall harken unto you and your shell shall be burnished. And when the fire ceases indeed, live you in supreme joy.

You shall not be alone in your adventure in this life—life *is* a wondrous adventure. I am always with you, for that which become I be the wind in its complete freedom. All you have to do is ask indeed and whatever desire you indeed do I quicken the way for you. But I shall not live your experiences for you, that you must do *yourself,* but to help you always, love you indeed always, allow you to know yourself indeed all ways [I shall]. *Never* consider yourself mere mortal again; [never] live in limitation again.

Do Not Preach To The World; The World Does Not Need Saving

Now—what have we done? We have opened that which is termed the gate and allowed great creatures to rush out into the world to try to change it? Nay! The world is weary of such creatures. You don't change anyone. What we have learned here this day indeed be that *your* truth, however you have accepted it, but allow everyone else's *there's*. And what do you become? Let it be a living standard that others can measure by. And never despise and not love or judge another, because what they be as their truth is not yours. Do not preach to this world—*live* in spite of it. And let everyone else be. The world doesn't need saving—leave it alone. *Indeed.*

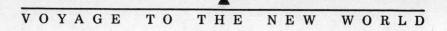

WEAR BOLDLY
THE
CARTOUCHE
OF YOU

TACKING MANEUVERS

What The Heck Is Heaven?

Millions of people throughout the world are seeking their psychic unlimitedness. What is it they are seeking? What are they finding? Many who have been surveyed have concluded that they are seeking a greater understanding of the world in which they live. Included under the major subject heading, *greater understanding,* are questions of how they are to interact with the people of that world, questions about their relationship with the universe and the God/Source of that universe, and questions about the possibilities of the unseen worlds beyond. We seem to be seeking a greater understanding of the complete creatures that we are.

Various elements of society have emerged to answer these ponderings: educational systems are re-tooling to satisfy this demand by pushing forward the boundaries of science and technology; societal systems are re-addressing issues of human rights, freedom, protectionism, interaction; religious systems are re-defining their differences into a "God is All" approach, yet they are still clinging tenaciously to the concept that their own particular brand of religion is the only way, the *only* truth.

"My Brand Is Better Than Your Brand"

Each religion's claims of, "Our path is the only path to Heaven," worked in the not-too-distant past for millions of believers. For today's sophisticated batch of seekers however, these claims of exclusivity on the pathway to Heaven simply do not compute. Many believe that all paths are the paths to Heaven, which does make a lot of sense. Since all religions define God as omnipresent—present in all things at all times—it would figure that God would be present in *all* seekers and, no matter what their path, it would lead to Heaven. Of course, this goes without saying what *Heaven* is or isn't.

Since it appears that religious philosophies are unable to satisfy the demands of this age's sophisticated thinkers, various spiritual organizations have emerged to take up the slack. Just as many people explore differing religions, many seekers travel about the world looking for that particular spiritual organization that represents their ideas of what life should be. Each spiritual organization offers a differing variety of ideals, philosophies, logic, concepts, rules, symbology; they offer the same basic structures as religion yet with their unique modifications.

Seekers select their spiritual organizations the same way millions of Americans select their faiths: by identification to value systems. We, as humans, identify with that which is most like the way we are, that which represents the values that we perceive and respect. From perceived values we develop belief systems, which are simply *How we think about that* systems.

Most religions and spiritual organizations maintain what is called a *lord.* The lord is usually the founder, the leader, the ideal, or the idol of that particular organization. As each seeker sees himself reflected in the lord of that particular religion or organization, an identity is established between the lord and the seeker. In essence, the seeker has aligned with that lord and is able to learn from that lord's teaching and value systems for a time. Eventually, as the seeker grows in his *own* unlimitedness, he begins to follow oneself.

Wear Boldly The Cartouche Of You

RAMTHA: That which you wear around your neck, how many beads does it possess?

MASTER: One hundred and six right now.

RAMTHA: And for that which is termed the cartouche to which it encompasses, whose cartouche is it?

MASTER: Bhagavan Sri Rajneesh.

RAMTHA: Ah! A wondrous entity. Do you feel that you are equal to this entity?

MASTER: Sometimes.

RAMTHA: Sometimes? What makes you unequal?

MASTER: When I'm not in the awareness of being that equal. When my awareness is limited.

RAMTHA: My wondrous Master. 'Tis a great truth you have learned many things. Perhaps the greatest thing that you have learned is to struggle for the desire of perfection. Struggle! That is a wondrous lesson indeed to learn; it is a virtue as it were. But you see, you are no equal match to anyone on any level, seen or unseen. It is unfair and highly presumptuous of yourself that you can equate the same ideal of perfection to any individual because it is not yours to equate to.

Let me tell you a great wisdom and you, of course, may have the grace to do with it whatever you wish to. You never become, ever, you never know God, ever, and you never know who you are, ever, as long as you follow another entity—*ever.* All you ever learn [are] the frustrations of attempts [at] being in the shadows of those ideals which were not precedented by you but precedented by another wondrous entity who has set them into motion, a beautiful God.

I tell you, your destiny, and that which is termed the endeavor of what is called life, is not to be as *anyone* else—that will never be—but to be the brilliant, blatant, arrogant, humble, all loving God that you are, that only you and your own truth can be. For what have you and what possess you? No one, seen or unseen, possesses greater. That is how it is. No one! You, if left alone without that which is termed the appeal of frustration in your life to be as others are, be highly creative, highly loving, humbled. [And if you are] motivated by the sheer simplicity that God the Father is you, you will make a happy life of this life and contribute to that which is termed the continuance of who be you in all this wonderfulness.

I beseech you, as that which is termed the brothern unto what is called the entity you, to learn to love, to accept, and to forgive what you are, wholly for you, and to hold yourself at high esteem. Follow what is termed the path of joy and enlightenment that your *own* emotional embodiment called the Soul has set into a precedence for you. If you go against it you will be in turmoil. When you wear the cartouche of another entity, which you do—in any form—you are giving all power to that entity and reserve to you none. That is why you have times of great limitedness and the furrows of sorrow.

It would be more God-like and more loving of your unlimited Christ of the unlimited Self to wear upon you boldly the cartouche of you, for what could be more divine in your own truth. And what is the true connection to God? It is not outside of you, Master, it is within you—it is called *you.* When you do this you give all the power back to you where it belongs. Then you are sovereign. As everyone strives to be sovereign they can only do it in the mimics of their own joy, in the mimics of their own illusion Self-created. That is where total happiness is.

You contemplate this. Contemplate it and the whole wisdom of your Soul—it will tell you what to do. Then you will never fail in this life—ever. You cannot fail, there is no such thing. You can only enhance the wisdom if allowed to do so. See?

MASTER: Is there anything that would be helpful for me to guide myself to myself?

RAMTHA: Absolutely! Cease trying to live by everyone else's standards, pious or unpious. *Everyone.* For everyone is exuberating their own individual truth to which *they* have set into precedent, and they have set it into a power. What you must do, Master, is to go within yourself and realize one thing—that the Source, the Divine Embodiment, God, if you will, has requested simply one thing from you and all others that are so gathered here, and that is to be happy. It is a term appropriately learned in your language but few understand it. It means joy. That, in itself, is the only request. And yet it holds a variable of complete unlimitedness which is God. God is not a limited faction: it is the continuance of forever.

Know you what the voice of God is? 'Tis not someone chattering at you, or written verbiage—it is none of those things. It is the emotion, it is electrified feeling within the Soul that makes you feel. That is the prize of life experience. Love yourself by listening to what you feel. Listen to how you feel about everything. And if the whole world disagrees with how you feel, love the world for exhibiting its own judgment and its own truth. Allow *them* to be without removing *you* from your decision based on your emotional body and how it feels. That is *true* love of Self.

And if everyone else is in agreement on any one, as you would term it, subject, only to please the whole of the group, and if it does not please you, do not judge them for it. Love them that they have exercised the option to be followers. And give yourself the grace to have your own objective truth. What greater thing and greater homage could you pay to the Father within you than by *being* you, living forth the innate destiny that was set into you eons, eons ago.

Sitting in mountain tops and monastories and caves and being a wretched entity of pious sovereign truth is boring and limited. Laughing with the wind, adoring lovers, listening to yourself, watching life's engagement; that is sheer joy, that is God. You learn by being free in that understanding. I will help you.

MASTER: Thank you.

RAMTHA: But take on no one else's image except *your* image, the [image of the God within you], aye? Why think you that I come forth in that which is termed the most outrageous manner as I do here, aye? You are listening to me but you see that which is termed my daughter's embodiment? Very good reason, Master. Everyone here has a tendency to follow anyone who has the word regardless of what it means. And yet, for eons you have been following everyone's specified truths to God and their images, thinking that would bring you closer. You don't listen very well.

Here there is no image, there is no face to hang upon your wall and to burn incense to. And there is no temple in which to go to be engaged in the spirit of the ideal of one entity. And there are no feet to kiss. My daughter would not be so conducive to let you do that to her feet. When you come here you will learn and it will happen. And when you leave you have no image of me—the only [image] you have is of yourself. And *that* is purposeful God; that is what this is all about. You see? I will be with you in the days of your time. All you have to do is ask—the wind, it will come to you. But you make all the decisions.

In This Moment You Can Change Your Entire Life

MASTER: This psychic friend I know seems to be able to see into the future.

RAMTHA: Everyone can do that. Everyone is what you call a psychic; everyone can see a future. All they have to do is see the attitude. Does it make you happy to see this wondrous entity?

MASTER: Yes it does. It makes me feel good.

RAMTHA: Are you learning or allowing her to teach you?

MASTER: I believe I'm learning.

RAMTHA: Do you not know you can do it yourself?

MASTER: Yes . . . but this seems like an easier way.

RAMTHA: If you feel this makes you happy to continue, by all means do continue, Entity. For if it pleases you then do so, but I will tell you this—that which another entity tells you, if you accept it and believe it, it will always come to pass, for you have created it yourself through that which is termed belief. That is the way it occurs. Entities who were once called seers [foretold the future]; those who were called prophets also did this and used their power, as it were indeed, to control nations and people.

If it makes you happy to do so then do it. But whatever you hear that does not please you, then do away with it or reject it. You are the creator of your destiny. This moment you can change your entire life, Entity, in a moment as you did with that which is termed hanging up your spirits. If one tells you this and this and this will happen and you believe it, it will. None has control over you save *you*—remember that.

If it brings you to light and there is good that is being seen, and the good is elongating you and making you more unlimited, then do continue. But remember that you are God too, and that you are on an equal basis. And what this entity is doing, so can you. Never forget that for then you are slipping into that which is termed the line of worship and following rather than becoming. So be it.

Into Freedom

RAMTHA: Let us talk of becoming. What shall you become unto? What have you been that you need thus to become? Who were you? Where did you issue forth from?

What is the reason for the issuing? And if you are to become, what be it shall you become that is so different from where you came from?

In becoming as it were indeed, it is not into that which is called the regulation of laws, into that which is termed dogma, constriction. Becoming, as it were indeed, is becoming without them into an essence of freedom, into that which is termed an expressive value that is able to express to the totality of the individualized entity without limitation. Becoming is unfolding in measure from limitation into unlimitedness. An entity that is immersed in that which is termed laughter, in joy, in happiness, has come forth in greater review, in greater understanding, when they relinquish limitation from their totality.

What shall you become? What is it are you becoming? Cloistered Self, Entity, is one that is wrapped in limitation and fear and that which is called superstition and law. An entity that is immersed within the flesh hath the limitation of that which is called the feeling of the flesh; needs and wants as it is seen. Coming unto unlimitedness is unraveling Self for that which is termed the Divine Preview of what you are in all understandings.

As High As The Value Of Thought Can Take You

What is it? Your bodies, they are a wonderful collection of work—all of you are. But the principle of that which is termed your essence body is as far and as vast and as deep and as high as the value of thought can take you. You are a Light Principle; you are unfolding to a feeling that could go beyond the senses of the body indeed, go beyond that which is termed the limitations of the flesh and traverse [into] Light, Principle[s] of Thought, greater civilizations.

God became Man in limitation, for he became [from] All That Was in his Isness into a small portion of knowingness constricted to that which is termed distance and reach and fervor of feeling. Yet, within the same strike he was able to immerse himself with mass and be a part of that which is termed creation, and feel and taste and touch and hear and speak and become glorious with this wondrous painting of that which is called Universal Creativity. From minute matter into great matter, can a thought embrace it? Nay! But a same vibration can. Thus God as it were indeed, the explicit creature of all that is, became singular, individualized, limited entity on this plane.

There Is More Than Flesh And Blood And Bone

We teach of becoming. The adventures of the body have been great—they will continue to be. The exploration of [the] truth of Self is an ongoingness. It excels each moment the entity rolls his eyes inward and begins to feel that which is termed the hearth of his being, begins to perceive the infiniteness of his beauty and begins to know there is more than that which is termed the collection of molecular structure that equates [with] that which is termed flesh and blood and bone.

We have taught of becoming for a good spell in your counting. Of becoming what? You are still of flesh. What have you become in the opening up? A *feeling* entity—an entity that goes beyond that which is termed the bodily feeling into *emotional* feeling. Emotion is not born of the body, it is explicitly *explained* in the body through that which is termed outward spasms of that which is termed the body convulsion. But emotion is born of that which is termed gratified thought felt in the conclusiveness of the entity and expressed in the body.

You have lived as nomads. You have lived as that which is termed the product of society, of change of consciousness. You have been the duplicatus of that which is termed the conscious ideal; all of you. Unfortunately that which is termed the ideal is a very limited, wretched entity that is prone to ailments, and sicknesses and neuroses and all things that inhibit that which is termed the becoming of the *individualized* Self.

Allowing The Individual Divinity To Occur Back Within Man

But what is born of that which is termed becoming? Emotion—deep, profound emotion. That is not the song of all society in the same wind. It whispers of ancient knowingness, of gratified now, of future perspectives, of reaching for a great star and beyond. Emotion allows the entity to do that. You do not become God until you become that which is termed the epitome of what is called emotion—to feel *profoundly*. Feeling allows the individual divinity to occur back within man; his Godhood replaced, his capstone replaced, his uniqueness in becoming.

We have become from a measure of likeness entities; of law and restriction into feeling—love, deep love, emotion, deep emotion, joy, deep sorrow, deep feelings of a weeping soul that knows not why it weeps, of tenderness, gentleness, compassion—what this plane would term humility is brought on in becoming. To be back unto that which is termed, as it were indeed, the Isness you cannot. To on go unto that which is termed its peak of being you can.

You are becoming in the moment by feeling. Everything that all here have done, hath struggled for, of designed experience, has been for that which is termed the virtue called emotion, for feelings. Your society has dictated what the ideals of feeling should be, and all strive to be it so that they are accepted. In becoming there is no ideal except what is felt deep within the individualized Self. Here, one gets in touch with his own premise, his own intelligence, his own purpose for being, his own good, and begins to feel it. The breaking away, as it [is] appropriately termed, [from] what is called the norm of society—its laws, its regulations, its petty ideals—becomes a war, a difficulty within the time of becoming, and all here are experiencing it.

And what shall you become? The body continues to elevate itself and refine itself; [it] will continue to become more valid and more useful to the great creative mind that sits within it. But 'tis the mind of collective value that is becoming more unlimited, and not through intellectual fervor but through that which is called emotion—deep emotion—profound Isness, God's reality, all that life is.

The Pulsing Of The Illusion

But what life is, in the semblance of its ideal, is an illusion. The pulsing of the illusion is the emotion called feelings that God's kingdom is made up of. The tree pulsates, the grasses pulsate indeed, the clouds pulsate, the waters pulsate, the flower in its budding bloom pulsates in color and hue and aroma. 'Tis these things that are cloaked in illusion [that] allow the true value of God in emotion to become prevalent and clear.

To become, one does not restrict himself from love and joy and feelings—*deep* feelings profoundly. He allows them to come forth for he is the stigma of that which is termed the virtue of God in feeling that gratifies us, that elevates us, gives us that which is termed purposeful value. Becoming—the body will continue to become, but that which is within it will become an all-knowing, all-feeling character of divine providence, divine beauty.

You Become One With All Great Things

Words often shall not describe that which is termed feeling; only emotion does, emotion that hath no value for it simply is. Then quiet becomes prevalent as it is in the heavens. Peace becomes prevalent. You become one with all great things that are ongoing and silent. Does the sun speak? No. Does a great star speak? No. A smaller? No. The moon? No. Do the trees speak? The plant? The bloom?

What speaks? God in his infinite Isness is *quiet* within the emotion of himself.

As you become the joy will overtake you, for the revelation of divine beauty seen within each of you shall become clear. Your beauty shall become profound. The limitations of arrogance shall dissipate from Self and Self shall become a feeling creature of Isness to what it really is. You'll begin to lose words to explain . . . feelings immerse and overtake and overcome, and the body begins to feel liftness within itself because that which is termed the grandest vibration is taking place within and cannot be uttered without.

All that I have taught you I shall continue to teach you, [to provide a] more profound learning of simplicity of those things you have not put into applicable principle. But you must know what you are going to become and where you have come from in order to steadfast your identity.

Everyone wants to know who they once were. It is of no import—they've all gone to make you what you are now; the creative adventurer ready for more adventure, ready for more feeling, more joy. God culminates himself into All That Is. When that which is emitted from himself, of thought, is felt and sent back to him, that is what you are.

What Use Is The Future Unless It is Now Felt?

In this year of yours to come, in its calendar of understanding,[1] we are putting, as it were indeed, a great electrical band around your earth. The band is to help steadfast and establish a polarity that is now beginning to occur upon your plane. The polarity shall be between joy and fear.

Fear is the dogma of religion, and of war and rumors of war, and of endings. And the dastardly entities that profoundly make it their knowingness are exacting Gods.

1. This discourse was delivered 22 November, 1981.

The other pole shall be in joy, of life, of loving the moment, of being, of the ongoingness of Isness. What is the tomorrow unless it is now seen? What use is a future unless it is now felt? If all things end this moment, it was felt this moment. Thus all things are completed now. The polarity will be a great pull. The band is a great blue light. We are cleaning the stratums and bringing balance to that which is termed your plane.

Joy exudes life, it draws life from all principle understandings. In joy, in peace you have not to utter a word but simply to feel; and it is the language of all things—feelings. In the year to come all of you in this room shall experience the heights and the widths and the depths and the breadths of that which is termed love and joy and feelings without words, of electrical emotions that electrify and explicate the being into another dimension.

And all will learn this. You *must* learn this in order to become out of your body a traveling entity that can immerse himself on other realms of realities. No one enters the gates of Heaven lest he hath love within his being, joy within his being—feeling. For what are the gates of Heaven indeed? They are made up of that which is termed as it were indeed the Isness. And all that prevail within are emotion.

Become The Child In Laughter

In order to become you must *feel* the becoming, and that we prepare in that which is termed in your year to come and for the rest of what is called this decade in your time. Be happy with that which you are. Fruitfully live in the moment. Feel—become, as it were indeed, the rose, become a lily in the field, become a trout in the stream. Become a great leaf who has changed its color; become the tree and how deep the roots go. Become the child in laughter and the wind on the water and the subtleness of a new bloom and the hopefulness of fruit.

Become all of these things—feel them, know them, become the Isness and love what you are and be a light unto yourself. And know you shall see the Kingdom of Heaven for all that it is—emotion. Those who fall in love when the moon turns to purple or when the wind blows through their hair, or when a twig falls to the ground, or when a bird takes flight, know about emotion. Thus they know about the enrichment of the God that they are and the virtue to which they have obtained to know that.

Learn to feel, to touch, to examine, to be—live in this and bless the Lord God of Your Being and the Father that is the Magnificence of All Magnificence and behold the splendor that you shall feel. When you perceive a life called Utopia, which is the promised land coming into full vista, coming into full view, all the mysteries they become resolved, all the superstitions are done away with, all of the dogmas of doom and destruction are no more. God reigns supreme over All That He Is and *He* is Life—the Ongoingness Isness. *That* no one take away. That is how it is.

Torment Your Self No More, You Are The Prince Of Peace

Torment yourself no more; do not be abusive to yourself any longer. Relinquish guilt. Do not live in a hurry, slow down and live in the moment. Do not live by rules, live by feelings. *Be.* Stop being another's ideal—be your own. Have peace with your body—torment it no more; starve it not into little or no-ness; love it and nourish it, it is a tender thing. And be liken unto no one else except what you are within your *unique,* individualized Self.

I beckon unto you, you are the Lord of Hosts, *you* are the Prince of Peace. Learn to *live* it, that the immaculate entity that presides within you is the immaculate entity now seen, not the duality that causes the confusion. Love yourself enough to speak highly of Self. Love yourself enough to live—to live in the moment, to exalt all that you are.

There Is A Tomorrow Coming

Do feel and love that which you feel, and live it in this moment, for it is that which is termed the director of moments to come. You are the tenders of a new age. Love and bless your Self—be tender unto yourself and live, for there is a tomorrow coming. Be glad for it. So be it.

LIVES
BEGIN
TO
BLOOM

FOG'S CLEARING, SIR

March, 1983

I suppose those of us who would sit in contemporary judgment of the value of a teacher would base our judgments on the teacher's *success* rate. Therefore, a number of people were interviewed at various locales in order to ascertain what benefit, if any, they have derived from the words, philosophies, and realities of the unseen entity Ramtha, The Enlightened One. Each interview told a unique story, and each story helped to uncover a little bit more of this enigma, Ramtha. Each interviewee discussed the particular stage of life that they felt they were in. Many were able to explain the person they were in comparison with the person they are now.

Each interview was an inner view into self; each person told of their understanding of the blooming of their lives. And each person expressed their truth perfectly, from the woman in her simplicity who sang a song of joy, to the gentleman with his intellect who wove a fabric of intense knowledge. The woman perhaps knew not of the man's intense quest for understanding, and the man perhaps knew not of the woman's simplicity in joy. Yet, the thread that wove through all of the interviews was the thread of discovering the grandeur of self.

Their viewpoints begin.

I Put My Self Back Into My Life

MASTER: How is Ramtha different from other teachers I've experienced? The others seem to tell you what to do, but they never tell you who you are. They may state that you are God but they certainly are not willing to provide the knowingness for you to discover it, to know it yourself. They *are* willing to state that you are God, and that your knowingness will emerge as you emerge through the worship of them.

I've never met anybody who could tell me what they are, who could convince me that they knew what they are, because nobody knew what they were. Ramtha *knows* what he is infinitely. And he has the ability to share his knowingness in unlimitedness. That is why he is able to explain *us,* to explain who we are. It's all very well for somebody to tell you, "You are God." Now, if you don't *know* God and you don't have an ideal for God, how do you know what that means? You don't have that knowingness because you have not experienced it. But with Ramtha, he opens the doors to the experience of Godness. God is an Isness, and I think of Isness as *Sense I.*

DOUGLAS: Where does *Sense I* come from?

MASTER: Put the mirror to *Isness* and you'll see, *ssensI.* Then say it, "ssensI." If you break the word down and spell it like you say it you have, "Sense I." That's the way I remember it. I remember Godness as *Sense I in totality.* Ramtha opened my eyes up to me. He is able to make you aware of the ideal that you are to yourself. You become aware of the ideal of your Self; you glean from the moment the potential that you are. You begin to gleam. That new unlimited consciousness that you are allows you the new understandings of your new unlimitedness. So, every time you think who you are, every time you sense your Self, you have a little bit more of knowingness to know what you know. Therefore you can experience your Self more, moment by moment.

When you say to somebody, "Love yourself," they have no idea what you're talking about. They think, *Why should I? How should I? What do I do to* love *my Self? Is that being selfish? I don't want to be selfish. Who am I? How can I* love *my Self?* By understanding who you are you learn to love your Self. When Ramtha sends you to *you,* you cannot help allowing the understanding to come. And then you walk away not even knowing why you feel happy, but you feel happy because the understanding of your Self is greater. And that, in itself, is the function of loving yourself.

The more understanding that you have of your Self, the more joy wells up in you, the more happiness is there within you. And when you are happy, in joy, you are living your Self. And when you're happy, how can you not like everyone else? Happiness is really an unconscious effort. Loving yourself is the knowing how to identify happiness, to know the cause of happiness, then to know the effect of happiness upon you and those around you. Happiness is the now-moment with God; happiness is the now-moment with Self.

I know a teacher that always says, "The difference between you and me is that I know I am God." Ramtha says, "The difference between you and me is that I know that I am God *and* I'm willing to show you that *you* are God." Ramtha allows you to visualize the manifestation of the truth. He allows you the joy of manifesting your own truth, the joy of manifesting your Godness, the experience, the realization in your life of what he means when he says, "You are God, too." That is what we benefit from.

One Day You Will Shine The Spotlight On You

If your life hasn't been working, even though you've worshipped, even though you've done everything that *they* have told you to do that will supposedly bring you happiness, just realize this—your followship is bringing *them* great happiness; you're helping *them* realize their Self. One day you will decide that you have spent enough time glorifying them and you will shine the spotlight on you and glorify you. As long as we cater to someone else's needs, thinking of their happiness more than of our own, we lose a piece of ourself for we have not given our Self that which we have given others; the Self feels very left out of your life.

Remember when you were a little kid, and you wanted to play a game with your friends but they didn't want to play with you? They left you out of their fun. Do you remember how you felt, how you cried, how the world had ended? That is how your Self feels when you leave your Self out of your life. I put my Self back into my life by simply loving my Self. I looked at my Self with love and respect—I talk to my Self, I tell my Self that I *love* Me. Ramtha is not a movement or a following or a fellowship. He is an understanding, a truth, a knowingness, a reality.

When You Are Happy You Have Everything You Desire

The Early Days

MASTER: When J.Z. was first channeling the Ram, her body was not vibrating at a frequency high enough to accommodate the movements that he often wished. So, at the first dialogues his eyes were closed but you didn't really notice it. I had forgotten about this until a friend reminded me the other day. And then he wouldn't move; he didn't move his arms, he would move his head by moving his upper torso. When J.Z.'s body became more able to accommodate his frequency he started using it more. I remember the first time he walked down the stairs, everyone gasped thinking, "When is he going to fall?" And then he looked indignant when people made a fuss about it. His speech mannerisms . . . he sounded like he hadn't spoken English for about six hundred years. It was very stilted and mannered, it was a lot of Old English sounding. And it was very difficult to understand him, I think mostly because of the physiological thing of manipulating J.Z.'s body to produce sounds—she still maybe resisted it; her body did, it wasn't accustomed to his frequency.

But also he wasn't able to express himself in such a contemporary manner as he does now. By being in the Dialogues and by being with people in their day-to-day lives, he has picked up all sorts of speech patterns and slang and euphemisms that he did not use at first because he hadn't been exposed to those words. He always says words have no meaning anyhow, and that you endow them with meaning in order to communicate. On the frequency level where he lives most of the time you just communicate thought and feeling. Here, we have to communicate using words when we really don't have to if we just knew that.

DOUGLAS: Where does Ramtha live most of the time?

MASTER: He refers to that all of the time as my home, or my place, or the Seventh he'll call it sometimes, or his Kingdom. And I'm not exactly sure where that is. He's described it to others in greater detail—describing his throne and his rooms and the food he has. It is a place other than this where everything is in alignment with the Father and it all comes directly from the Source. It's a place of seventh level understanding, whatever that means to you. It means something different to everyone but it sounds wonderful.

DOUGLAS: What do you think Ramtha is?

MASTER: What is he? Well, I can tell you what he is to me. I can't speak for anyone else. To me, the first time I ever met Ramtha—and this goes the same thing for the first time I met J.Z.—it was a very deep recognition. It was like seeing someone that I have known forever and has been very important to me forever. And to see them in this plane and this dimension was astounding—it ripped me, pulled me loose and threw me all over.

And, to me, Ramtha's very much a God/man because I can see him how he is when he is in his body. I remember that; what he was like when he was walking on this plane and he's very much—I don't want to say human, because none of us are human, we're all Gods—but he has that *humanity* that we know up here and he exposes it all of the time and reveals it; and I see it all of the time so I feel very personal with him, like he is a friend just like we're sitting here talking, I always feel that.

To me he's the Ram, he's Joe, he's a guy you know. And then, on the other hand, when I see him in action I still am just in awe of him because of his facility with language now; and with dealing with everyone in the moment and knowing them, and dealing with every person however trivial it may sound to me. I'm amazed to see him really feel what that person is feeling, and how he becomes them so that he knows what they are really asking. All he knows in the moment is *that* person and their needs. To me, that is just so astounding. I've never seen anyone do that.

I'm not afraid of him anymore. I always was for a long time but now I feel very comfortable with him and can be who I am. And that's also because I love and know myself now that I can do that also. I can do it with anybody but especially with him because I don't feel a separation—I feel that he and I are one and that I am no different than he.

I know a lot of people still feel that Ramtha is *the* Ram, like he is a deity, he's this great teacher, he's this Master, someone you come to and sit at his feet. They don't feel like they are capable of being what he is. They've made him their ideal but they themselves don't realize that *they* are their own ideal and that he became who he is today through all his lessons and his trials and his fires. That, we all do; I know that it's so for me and for him. I have very much a feeling of ease with him. That's who the Ram is to me.

DOUGLAS: Do you know how he reads people?

MASTER: Just like I was referring to, he literally *becomes* them. If, in a quiet moment in contemplation . . . let's say you are in your own home and you would sit down with an object, a flower or a stone or anything, a thing of beauty or whatever, and if you look at it and contemplate it you really start *becoming* it because that is the only way you *know* anything, by becoming it. You don't know any *thing* by looking upon it; you only know a thing by becoming it. If I had a rose in my hand and I looked at it, I would know that its petals are soft and what its color was because I felt the vibration of the emotion that that flower was given and has through thought. And that's what the Ram does.

For those who sit in the gatherings he says he looks into their Souls or into their *books*. He feels all the multi-dimensional emotions one has and he is also able to attach wisdom to those feelings so he really knows what their *complete* experience is. And since he's not ruled by time or space, he can go back to the day they were born in this lifetime and live their whole life in one moment because time is a no thing for him. He can step outside of this plane, this dimension, and experience someone's whole life or all their lifetimes.

He might pick one which the person's referring to, or he might pick a lifetime eight hundred years ago which is the person's challenge in their life at this time—he will just flip to that and experience that. To the gathering, it is just a moment that he has paused, but he's gone all the way across the globe and maybe to other galaxies to catch the light—and back and forth—and into different bodies and dimensions to answer someone's question. And so, he *really* knows. You could go to a Gypsy psychic and they "know," but it is on a much more limited reality-truth than what Ramtha can experience.

DOUGLAS: You have attended scores of Ramtha Dialogues. How would you summarize those millions of words you have heard?

MASTER: This is something that I think about a lot when I run. With running, a lot of unlimited thoughts can come in. The Ram has told us everything from the start. To get it, it's not a matter of listening to three hundred tapes or going to a hundred Dialogues, because in one sentence, in one moment, he always says what the key is to this whole wonderful mystery and game that life is. He's always said it in just one word and it's so utterly simple that nobody understands it; and they keep waiting for him to tell us this big secret like, how do you transcend this plane into a realm of total unlimitedness? How would I summarize all three hundred tapes? You see, I would start by using too many words.

DOUGLAS: We were trying this yesterday; we started with three words, then two, then one.

MASTER: Yes, I want to say, "Live and be happy," or "I Am Joy," or, "I Am," or "Be". . . any of those. That is the answer to anything and everything. And all my contemplations and challenges keep coming back to that because with that, with the state of Beingness and Isness, comes happiness and joy, and with *that* comes the answers to everything. And when you're happy you are free; and when you are happy you are allowing the hormones from your ductless glands to start secreting in your body so that it opens up more of your brain so that more unlimited thought does come in. By just *living* you experience everything that you have set up when you came into this experience. And you came into this experience to learn and experience that which you need.

Life Is A Setup

When you are happy you are at one with the Father; you do not experience a duality which is what gets us into trouble all of the time, feeling a duality. That's what atonement is, at-onement. When you are happy, which comes from being, Isness, the *I Am,* you have everything you desire because that is the law; that is *The Way It Is.* We set it up. We're the Gods that created everything and that's how we said it should be. And it's always worked, it always has, even in all of our miseries and all of our lifetimes. Everything we have said and thought has come to us and that's why we have been miserable. Or we've judged those things thinking, *that's misery,* or, *that's unhappiness.* But when you are just living and being you, you do not judge your thoughts and so everything is just perfect, every thing just is.

DOUGLAS: I wanted to put in here to explore, when you said that Ramtha *becomes* us when he communicates with us, perhaps that is his beingness, his concept of beingness?

MASTER: Well, also, he speaks about all of us being the plural expression of the Father. We all are the same. We're all the Father, meaning we're singular yet plural. And so he doesn't know a division between himself and the other Gods. That's probably why he uses singular words when it would be grammatically correct to use plurals; he doesn't know a division. And that's maybe another way he becomes, experiences someone, because he knows that we are one because we are *all* the Father. But that's something which I don't quite understand yet.

DOUGLAS: That we are another experience for him?

MASTER: We *are* him and he is *me.* We *all are the* same thing, we are the same creation of the Father. Probably because of his knowingness he is able to be one with all things and, of course, when you *are,* you have access to all knowledge and emotion and all time. Perhaps all knowledge and emotion and time condenses into this big ball of Isness that he accesses in the now. To him, past, present and future all exist in that big ball. That's probably why, when he speaks, he mixes up past tense with present tense and with future tense; to Ramtha there is no difference.

DOUGLAS: How would you summarize Ramtha's truth in no words?

MASTER: In no words? Just a real belly-laugh! Just a great, big, "HAAAAA!"

DOUGLAS: A big belly-laugh, aye? Well then, in discussing the concept of the *I AM,* how do you see loving yourself?

MASTER: It's kind of a *Catch 22* or a circle thing, but in that state of Isness you cannot help loving yourself because in just being you do not judge anything; every *thing* just is. So therefore, you would not be judging your Self so you could not but help love your Self in that context.

DOUGLAS: The word *love* is difficult to define in today's contexts.

MASTER: Indeed. I think of love as a limitation also because there is something even more than love. In the modern Christian doctrines, and in so many of the eastern guruisms, love is expressed as an end in itself. But love is just a means—not just a means, it's more than that—but it's a means to coming to a state of Isness.

So many teachers bring people to this feeling of feeling wonderful, of feeling love in their Fourth Seal; opening that up but they do not go beyond to the Fifth Seal of Manifestations, or the Sixth of Seeing the Father in All Things, and the Seventh of Becoming the Father in All Things. Once those teachers help you to open up your

Fourth Seal they step right in for the closing—they sell you on *their* symbol of the divine instead of telling you that it was *you* that felt that marvelous feeling so therefore *you* should be *your* symbol of the divine. It's funny—once they open your feelings up to love they close you right back down into limitation.

On The Way To The "HEY!"

That is such a basic early lesson, I know for me it was. I really didn't *love* my Self, and the Ram started teaching me that by incredible lessons of fire—fire after fire after fire, and challenges and challenges, and stripping myself bare 'til I *had* to see my Self—and I saw the . . . *Hey!* [In exclamation] I saw the God within me and that's when I really began to love my Self. I mean, *unqualified* love.

DOUGLAS: Some of the steps on the way to a state of being.

MASTER: When you say, "on the way to," that makes it a duality already because that makes it into a linear, saying that there is a start and then you have to go to Point A, Point B, Point C. It's a much more unlimited thought, a much more unlimited emotion, than those thoughts and emotions that deal with making money, or satisfying your loins, or fighting someone. It's definitely greater than that.

A Lover's Symptoms

DOUGLAS: I would like to know, how do you know you *love* your Self?

MASTER: There are symptoms. Your body responds to it. You start becoming much healthier and have a greater ease of movement; your eyes are clearer; you laugh a lot; you enjoy being solitary because you get to experience yourself without having others there to block, just experiencing you and you enjoy it. When you can sit down with yourself for a whole day, or let alone for a week, and enjoy it. You must love yourself otherwise you couldn't stand being alone.

In New York, where I lived for years, most people I know are *never* alone. They're alone when they have to run home to change their clothes and take a shower before they run somewhere else. I don't know what would happen if they ever were alone. Perhaps everything would move in on them and that's why they never are alone, because they know what that would be like and they are protecting themselves from their Self.

DOUGLAS: What else? What are the other symptoms of a lover of Self?

MASTER: Oh . . . well, when you love your Self and then when you *express* that love, that's going into another realm. That would be the Fifth Plane and that is also the *paradise,* the Plane of Manifestation. If you loved your Self and if you expressed that love to your Self by being good to your Self, by not denying your Self anything you want—pampering your Self; good wine, nice clothes, whatever it means to you to express that love to your Self—that takes you into the whole next plane of the Fifth. That also means loving others also and so that would start opening up; that would mean the Fifth Plane, you would start manifesting. It takes loving your Self to do that.

DOUGLAS: So, being aware of your manifestations, viewing that which you manifest, is a hint that you're beginning to love your Self?

MASTER: I would think so. You're asking me something I've never really thought of in those terms—*what does it mean to* love *your Self? How do you know if you* love *yourself?* I suppose you would be happy—happiness to most people is a no thing, they don't know what it is. That's something that I just learned recently, what it is.

DOUGLAS: What is it?

MASTER: A big smile.

DOUGLAS: Do you say anything to your Self? What do you do? Do you say you love your Self?

MASTER: Do I say, "I love Me?" All the time. I'll pour myself a glass of wine and stand in front of the mirror and look at myself and just revel in my light and who I am, and drink down the wine. Every morning when I awake and every night before I sleep, I speak to myself telling myself how much I love me. When you bathe yourself in the light of your love, when you can *feel* yourself and can *accept* yourself, you know that this is wonderful, this *thing* that you have created.

DOUGLAS: In the days of the past, when we looked in the mirror and, in comparison with others, we looked upon our Self in a less than loving eye, was that hate of Self?

MASTER: That is judgment of Self.

DOUGLAS: Ah . . . so when we can say, "I'm overweight and it's okay, I love me regardless!" that is a judgment that hasn't been turned into hate for Self.

MASTER: Yes . . . that is a truth, but you are still judging your Self. It is when you say, "I love me the way I am!"—that is when you are *loving* Self. When you said, "I am overweight," that was a judgment of Self—you are comparing yourself to another who you think is at a perfect weight, and you are *over* that weight. When you can look at yourself and not see anything wrong with Self, *then* you are loving Self. When you're at that place, everything just *is*, and you just see it as it is.

DOUGLAS: One person interviewed said that you start taking a mirror to bed with you. In other words, you don't need to desperately look for yourself in other relationships anymore. There isn't that urgency to find your Self in other people. That desperate search to find fulfillment through another takes on a different attitude.

MASTER: I can see why—you can get cut real bad if you take a mirror to bed with you.

DOUGLAS: [Laughter] That's true. And you can be "cut" real bad if you are in desperate straits to experience your Self in another.

MASTER: Well, Ramtha constantly says, "You can't know what love of another is until you know love of your Self."

DOUGLAS: How have Ramtha's truths changed? And how have those who have listened to Ramtha's truths changed?

MASTER: [A jolly belly laugh] My . . . that's a complicated question.

Well, his truths have never changed. Since the first time I ever saw him, and I think others who have been around hearing him a long time would say the same thing, his truths haven't changed. He's always, in all ways, said the same thing. But the more we know and experience these teachings, the more we understand. It's seemingly brand new to us, but it's only new because we ourselves have grown and are brand new, we have allowed more unlimited thought to come in, including his unlimited teachings. It's just like the more I grow, the more I understand, the more I see what's there. So I can always keep taking.

As far as the Dialogues go, the format of the questions now are very different. It seems like they are all punches now—every question asked carries a grand impact, and every question receives an answer that carries grand impact. I can tell you when the Dialogues used to go all day and into the evening, and well into the night sometimes; everyone would keep asking the same basic question.

Every question is important—whatever you are dealing with in that moment and you ask him, he will be even with you and answer because he knows that's what you need in that moment. He doesn't judge one question as being more, as we would term it, profound or unlimited because it just depends where you are in *your* becoming.

Now, I think people come to the Dialogues already with so much knowledge and so much more light. I believe the consciousness of this plane is being lifted so much by his teachings and by all of us, all the thousands of people who have shared in his gatherings around the country, as well as people who have never been to any teacher, or to them their teacher is Joe down at the market. We learn from all sorts of people as well as from other established teachers. Ramtha puts everyone through the fire and makes you expand to meet that information and become more un-limited. The consciousness *has* been raised.

We've Been Hummin' Ever Since

MISTER X: I've gone through so much growing and developing, becoming of who I am, in the nine-plus months that I've been involved and around the Ramtha thing. There's been more dynamic interplay between me and other people, between me and life in general. I've become more alive, I've changed my entire lifestyle. I've gone from one who has possessed things and wanted to possess things to someone who possesses me. I've got me, man! And I'm happier now than I've ever been, ever.

MISTER Y: You were saying about the fire, it's gotten to the point where now I almost welcome it because I know how good I feel after I've gone through it. And I kick and scream all the way, "I don't want it, I don't want it," and then the *Ah's* come, the relief of living through another experience of you and seeing the beauty come through.

DOUGLAS: Ah . . . it hurts so good.

MISTER Y: No! When it hurts, *it HURTS!* Ramtha told me once, "For this learning you would do well to experience such a thing as this." And when you go through the experience, both you and the Ram are sitting there and laughing about it, smirking about it; and yet your conscious altered ego Self is there observing this gaiety over its pride. And then after it's all over you just take your learnings and laugh about the rest of it and go on.

MISTER X: I've had to overcome the thought of the here and the now, the physical reality, being other than a real important thing. And you find yourself getting sucked into it, "Where is my next meal going to come from? How will I pay my rent this month?" Now, when the money runs out, I don't think about that. Instead I think, *I'm being taken care of, I'm safe, there's no problem, I'm a manifesting God, this lacking doesn't matter.* And it's easy for me to say right now, I have eighty dollars in my pocket. But you might want to talk to me when I'm down to ten.

DOUGLAS: How has your life changed since you have been exposed to the teachings of Ramtha?

MISTER Y: Drastically! Well, wait a minute . . . drastic denotes an immediate turnover but it was not quite that way; it's been abrupt, though. I was pretty much on a Self-destruct mode until I met him. I let go of so many fears; I was afraid to be who I was and to express my own inner-being because I was real concerned with the eyes of the world, I was real concerned with what others thought of me. I thought I had to be a certain way to be acceptable. If that is still a part of my being, it is submerged under layers and layers that I have yet to peel off. Ramtha talks about a lifetime in a season and I know what that means.

MISTER X: A lifetime in a week! How have I changed? I had been studying everything there was to study. I was in my own little *looking to find God* shell, hiding behind my layers. I had been playing with metaphysical stuff and kind of desired it to be that way. Then I started talking to this person about "the Ram." I said, "Hey . . . come on, the *Ram?* You can figure out a better name than that." There was no way, I just wasn't believin' it. I said, "I know about transmediums—I know Jubal and then there's Seth and there have been a couple of others who have come into my life. And it's all right . . . it's okay to pass a Saturday night with, but it was nothing that was really that far reaching and nothing that I don't basically know myself somewhere."

And then I started listening to Ramtha tapes and reading the portfolio, and I saw that there was something more here. Ramtha *far* excels anything that I have ever heard and I have read the best of them. At that point in time I had read everything that Seth had put out. Ramtha touched things simply that Seth had put out in long, flowery, verbose kinds of terms. Ramtha just cuts right through the meaningless to the meaningful and gets right to it, the way it is.

Ramtha struck a cord with me and that cord has been hummin' ever since. It's like a rhythm that I've fallen into. I gave up marijuana, I gave up cigarette smoking, hard liquor—no sweat! I had been trying to give up smoking for ten or fifteen years. When I came in contact with some of Ramtha's truths—I read that portfolio about the grape and the weed—it really made sense to me, *I'm really killing myself.* Done . . . I quit. No sweat, no fire—that was easy.

MISTER Y: I, like you, was into the metaphysical stuff. I had read all of the Edgar Cayce stuff and I was real big into Castaneda; and I read all that stuff and I really mentally toyed with it, and I thought about reincarnation and I had done that for years and years. That which is different about the Ram is that you become an active living of it instead of a dry philosophical thinking about it.

167

MISTER X: And another thing that I like about Ram is that he doesn't ask you to do anything that he hasn't done himself. And he says he is not like other teachers, he's not going to draw you up to a certain point and then leave you in a devoteeship. You are going to be a God—you *are* a God, you just don't realize it, but you *are* going to realize it and become the fullness of your Godhood. There is nothing that he can't do, and that is in the realm within each and everyone of us.

MISTER Y: The things he says and the truth he speaks, we've all known it for so long in the infinite part of our being. He is the first one and the only one I've found that can speak that truth so coherently, so evenly. When I heard the things he said, it rang so true because I've known it all along and I've thought it all along, yet I never knew how to put it into words and I never knew how to put it into action, or at least, I didn't think I knew. It was so refreshing to have all of it put together for me.

No Trades Accepted

I had this armor of illusions that I wore—I was a rough guy and I didn't mess with emotions. The only emotions that were okay was to get mad, to hate somebody, and to have a lover. Those were my emotions. The other emotions were a no thing. From a barbarian I turned into a poet. I had written some poetry when I was a teenager, but then it wasn't *cool* to feel. Since I've met the Ram, I've met the treasure of myself. And I have found it through the sensitivity of feelings.

The only thing that can accelerate me more than the Ram, than to hear the things he said, is to read some of the things that I have written. I wouldn't trade any of this for anything. He said I would look back upon these days a..d that they would be worth it all; that everything that I had ever done was worth it to get to where I was at that point.

That felt so good all the way through me; to look back on everything that I had done—even all of the things that I felt guilty about and tormented myself about—that they were worth it all to get to that point.

MISTER X: And there has never been anything more painful, there has never been anything that I have felt more acutely and have gone through more divine fire over—wrenching me away from thirty-seven years' worth of dogma, teachings, being under the system's thumb, under your parent's thumb, the church's thumb, the school's thumb ... you name it. To suddenly be able to say, "Hey ... it's all a no thing; that's *their* truth, it has nothing to do with what I believe in; it has nothing to do with who and what I am, and what I am is a wonderful entity." I am really appreciative of what I've gone through and who I am. And I am saying that in all humbleness.

And every other person that I have met is a God unto his own being, each and every one of them. On my journey to Nepal, that was probably one of the biggest eye-openers that I had. Most of the people over there are illiterate but they are all getting by, they are taken care of. And each and every one of them is a God. And you would look in their eyes and be able to see that light. The light, to me, seemed brighter than many people I've seen in the States; those people who won't even look you directly in the eye because they feel like they are worthless.

And it is funny, isn't it—we go to church on Sunday and pay our tithes but we don't get anything out of it other than a big case of fear and guilt. Over there they just look up at you in these big brown eyes and you can see the light; it's in every one of those little faces over there. Even though their bodies are naked, they are clothed in the light of love. They've all got the light.

MISTER Y: I used to be so judgmental of people—everybody—everybody who wasn't in a real narrow, restrictive type that I felt was what I should be. But I learned it's real dangerous to judge others 'cause it's *your* Self that you are judging. What you judge is what you see in them that you don't like. And the only way for you to see it in them is if it's in you. So what you don't like in them, you don't like in you. When you "damn them," you damn *you.* The most valuable thing anybody can ever acquire or can ever learn is to *love* themselves and to be at peace with their Self. Ramtha is teaching me that. And there is no price, no value I could put on that. The more I feel comfortable and love my Self, the more I realize how deep my wisdom goes. There is no price for the wealth of Self.

MISTER X: Ramtha says he will teach you what *love* is, but we don't know what love is and we are just now learning. I don't even think we've started scratching the surface. The knowingness of love is a diamond in the rough.

MISTER Y: You know, I used to think I had to be so hard-nosed that I brought forth so many wrenching experiences and, in the process, blocked so many enriching experiences. Now, I've found enrichment in the simplest things—the vision of a child, the wisdom of a white-haired woman—the beauty of the sight just makes me cry. All these new emotions are so wonderful to experience, and I now know that in the past I was blocking them from my being.

MISTER X: I wasn't worthy of them, I wasn't worthy of gettin' it. I didn't see myself as being worthy of being loved by anybody, much less myself. I am now . . . *I AM NOW!*

Reflections On Self

MASTER: My impressions of Ramtha? The first time I met Ramtha was through tapes. My roommate had brought home a tape and on it was this strange sounding voice. I didn't think very much of it at first. I started to listen to it; I listened very, very intently. Someone lent us one hundred Ramtha tapes and we listened to every tape.

DOUGLAS: You listened to one hundred tapes?

MASTER: We listened to *every* tape for about three months. My roommate told me that we could actually meet this entity. I said, "We can meet *this* entity?!" And for me to hear Ramtha was to be touched, to hear his words. So, it was day and night of Ramtha tapes. I could hear Ramtha's voice in my ears very well after that. I began to talk to him and he would talk back, and his voice was the voice I heard on the tapes. We were talking before I even met him.

When I finally did meet him, the first thing he ever said to me was, "Master, I heard." I asked, "You mean I don't have to say anything?" He smiled, "No." The first time I saw him come out on the stage it was as if I was seeing myself, but my Self as *all* it could be, without any restrictions—he was *him* totally. I was touched . . . I was touched by myself. So, we didn't say very much in that first Dialogue, actually time kept me quiet. He told me to move to Oregon. I spent seven months on the Oregon coast. He told me to learn how to listen to the grass grow, to watch the trees be.

DOUGLAS: What is Ramtha to you?

MASTER: He is a mirror, he mirrors my totality. He is the only one I know who can do that. So, when I see him, I see my Self. He has been teaching me. And I'm quite clear about the lessons that come my way and the understandings that I come to. While I certainly give Ramtha credit, it's also me—my *Self* talking to me. On the inner level there isn't really a difference, there is only *one* God. We may have different vantage points—each one of us, I guess, is a different vantage point of the one God. He is where I am going, what I'm becoming; not that I become him but that I become all that I can be. That's what I feel he's done. He is *him.* He calls it *outrageous,* and I agree—he is outrageously himself in the midst of all of this.

DOUGLAS: How long have you been attending Dialogues?

MASTER: About a year and half now.

DOUGLAS: How have you changed?

MASTER: Immensely.

DOUGLAS: What do you know now that you didn't know then?

MASTER: Nothing. It's not so much more that I know, it's how much I've dropped off. I've dropped off lots of knowledge that limits, that cloaks. I already know everything there is to know. It's quite simple, it's just a matter of unknowing all of the things that have covered that up. The last step for me, now that I know what I am, is to *be* that and express it through the body. It's one thing to know it but I need to *be* that—all that I am—and let it shine out through my Self, so to speak. It just doesn't remain an ethereal type of knowing but becomes a reality in this body. That's a little more difficult.

DOUGLAS: Putting the knowingness into action?

MASTER: It's not so much action—*being* in this body and letting my Self shine through it. I have spent most of my life hovering about five feet above my body, watching it go through all sorts of things, not being a totality part of it. Conversely, for my Self to come into my body and to feel and to not abandon it, so to speak, to not allow my body to just care for itself but to *be* it, to give it my knowingness and my strength and my power; to let my Self shine through my body. Sometimes we become spectators to our Self—we don't do very much to help us.

DOUGLAS: Do you feel better about your Self or worse, or indifferent?

MASTER: All of those things, and much more than I used to. I'm going through a bit of fire now. I've spent most of the time I was out here with my roommate. We've been going through our fire together and that's familiar to me, I've done a lot of that. But this is the first time I'm doing it by myself for a while. What I have been thinking about is mirrors. I came from New York City. There were just hundreds of people I could mirror off of. I was a therapist there. There was always emotion and things for me to see myself in and for me to convince myself that *I am*, and that I am all of those things that I see in other people, the power, the emotion. I found myself out here being very dependent on those mirrors, that if they weren't around I wasn't feeling very powerful at all.

In some way, I am grieving the loss of all of those mirrors. Just from the energy of this Dialogue, what I've been feeling is to not need the mirrors so much but to just be what I am—to know what I am and then be it. I've been dependent on other people to create the energy for me and then mirror off of it. I am now growing to be dependent on my Self.

DOUGLAS: Is that how you feel you have grown?

MASTER: Yes, I have grown quite a large bit. As I said, I'm becoming my own source. That is the change that I am going through. I am the source, then I don't need to look outside for it.

DOUGLAS: My appreciation to you—I am grateful for this interview of you.

MASTER: It is fun, isn't it—talking, reflecting on Self. I always enjoy an opportunity to be me.

No Now Or Never

[At a restaurant somewhere in Seattle]

DINER X: Life is a scavenger hunt—you're always looking for the next clue that will carry you to the next step.

DOUGLAS: How do you know you're making headway?

DINER X: You don't have that *I'm lost* look anymore. You don't look in the mirror in the morning with that, *I'm lost* look. You have the *I am found* look.

DOUGLAS: And what have you found?

DINER X: There is no right or wrong, no now or never. There is just an Isness. What you want to do with it is totally your prerogative. Just *know* that you know.

DINER Y: It's not so easy to soar like an eagle when you're flying with a bunch of turkeys.

DINER Z: Everybody knows deep down in their Soul their Godness. They don't buy the garbage anymore. That which touches someone, that which lives in truth, is what is yearned for now. Enslavers will cease to exist when there is no one who will allow themselves to be enslaved.

The Promise Of All The Realities Of Tomorrow
An Interview With J.Z. Knight

DOUGLAS: J.Z., what is Ramtha?

J.Z.: [Following a long pause] He is a God who became a man; and through the herald of a life spent in discovery of his divine Self, became a God again. Ramtha, the man or the ego-identity that we identify with, is only the memory of the man. That which speaks through it is the God, alpha and omega, the beginning and the end, and the all-ways-is omnipresent understanding. Ramtha is an absurd enigma that is the promise of all the realities of tomorrow.

DOUGLAS: After living his teaching for five years during your becoming process, how would you summarize all of those words, those millions of words that have been spoken through you?

J.Z.: For me, personally? They were needed. What Ramtha is communicating will probably take a million words to get a single understanding across to where it is liveable—that I am a God that is not helpless against reality, but I am a God who must remember that *I* have *created* the reality. And in that understanding, I have deduced from that the power to outwit reality and make it whatever I want to. Thus, *becoming* would be to release one's narrow vision to allow him to see that *he* is responsible for everything that he is and ever will be. And, given that kind of information, then instead of saying, "Well, that's simply the way my life is," I can say, "That is *how* my life is and it is always subject to change and *I* have the ability to change it."

People think that *this* is the only reality, that they are doomed to unhappiness and they are doomed to the primeval instincts of survival. Anything can survive, anything. Everything survives. But to be here merely as a *survivor,* creation would not flower and bloom to the beauty and the extent that it can if we only existed for survival. Being here must be because, *from* the premise of survival we can become unlimited. And in that survival instinct, we can create joy and beauty and unlimited charisma through which we can express. We have to know that we are more than mere mortals, that we are the *great* immortals, that we are the designer of that which we have beseeched upon our Self. And we can redesign the picture any way we want to.

When people finally realize that they are caught in this hypnotic trance, when they come back into the true reality, *that* is when the Kingdom of Heaven will once again appear upon this and all other planes. My becoming is that I realized that that is a truth. And that's a long way becoming. You can't *become* unless you realize that you have the option to do it. For the next step, for me, is to have an adventure in my life now that I realize that that's *that* truth. Then it's living the dream according to my own design. That is what I am busy doing.

DOUGLAS: What is the one thing that you remember that makes you feel as a God? What is that one thing that we just keep forgetting?

J.Z.: We are very poor influences on ourselves into greatness because we have been intimidated into a lowered life form. In recent contemporary times, for two thousand years, we have been called *sinful creatures.* That stigma automatically takes away our ability to remind ourselves that we are great, or that we are equal with God or Christ or Buddha, or whomever. So *we're very terrible.*

Because of this onslaught, we've been very poor instruments in reminding ourselves of our greatness. The one that reminds us is the God that is within us, if that is allowed to be listened to. For me, it has been Ramtha who reminds me because I have a very bad habit, almost a hypnotic influence, of thinking that I am unworthy of things. That feeling of *unworthiness* evolves from two thousand years of being born into bodies in countries wherein the religion or the consciousness of the time teaches subservience. So, we have to come out of that and realize that we are worthy.

The one great thing that Ramtha does is that he will tell us, in three million words, in great repetition, tirelessly, that we *are* worthy until we ourselves feel worthy enough to tell ourselves of our worthiness. Ramtha is the one who reminds us. That's one wonderful thing that he has done for the people who have come to the gatherings. He has made us worthy of love, joy, happiness, and God; he has made us worthy of our Godness because we have been taught to be unworthy. We have been God's enslaved and that enslavement is in our cell memory, it is in our Soul memory, it is in our consciousness.

DOUGLAS: Is there a plan that Ramtha is using in terms of the unfoldment of his teachings?

J.Z.: I think the plan is that he is teaching, number one, to love. When they are capable of loving themselves, then they are capable of loving and understanding everyone else whom for so long they felt they had to live for. Then they don't have to live for them any more, they can live for themselves.

Number two, that this truth can be a demonstrated, manifested truth, that is not a prophesy per se for some untold generation yet to live and never in our time. This truth is to be lived *now* to where this truth becomes, not only a word *truth* and a philosophy, but can become the foundation of a whole life. And by the masters living this unlimited understanding means that it is possible to do this. In essence, that is what the Ram is teaching here, but he says, "Leave the world alone." They don't need saving—all they need is a good example, that's all. And by being that example, by living and becoming innovative in a day-to-day routine, the rest of the world will catch on. He is a grand strategist; he knows how to present it well.

DOUGLAS: Ramtha, in our simplicity, wants us to be what we are. What, to you, is this essence of becoming?

J.Z.: In how many words?

DOUGLAS: In three, four, or five.

J.Z.: I think the appropriate answer to this question is, there are no words to becoming. There aren't. You are speaking of general unfoldment and that denotes the absence of unique individual persons, the sovereignty of each individual entity. Yet, each individual entity's unfoldment is going to be much different than yours or mine or anyone else's. There are not words to becoming-ness—it is an Isness living process. No one has asked the question, "What are you going to be when you unfold? What is becoming? What is the creature that is the ideal?" We tend to say, "This is what you become—you *become* God." But to a person who is trying to obtain an ideal, what is it they are going to attain at the end of becoming?

Becoming is a whole, wonderful process which has been difficult to understand. What it really is, is a simplicity of *allowing* one's Self the virtue of living day to day, unobstructed by anyone else's views and laws and opinions. And so, what will be the end result of that? That each entity finally realizes that they *are* important. And that their own opinion and that their own ability to be God is really themselves. And it only takes *living* to convince a person of that.

After becoming themselves? Well, imagine a person in a lawless universe and the magical Source all around.

Imagine them creating, evolving, being whatever they want to be without any restrictions; then you have conceived the ideal of God/Man. But *that* has to be lived. That is something yet to be lived.

DOUGLAS: Your definition is simple yet complex. What are the symptoms of becoming?

J.Z.: Humility, forgivingness, allowing, a free-thinking process. An outward symptom you will see is the disapproval of people around you because they have always seen you in one mode of existence for so long.

A clear symptom is a change in one's opinion from the overall accepted attitude—the *everybody wears alligator shirts* attitude changes; it changes from being a reflection of social consciousness to a reflection of individual consciousness. That is the greatest sign of all. All of a sudden, instead of going with the flow of peoples' thoughts, fashions, and modes to exemplify acceptance, one exemplifies it within his own personal ideal unaffected by the whole group.

And, of course, one of the main symptoms is pure happiness.

DOUGLAS: The big smile.

J.Z.: Do you know that people literally can become happy if you leave them alone and you don't inflict upon them your ideals and opinions? And there is one other very important ingredient to happiness. If people *know* God loves them, that creates happiness in people. It doesn't matter if they love Him; it doesn't matter how they think they've been in their life or how they are, because how they are isn't important; if they *know* that God is going to love them regardless, that creates happiness in people. And you only receive that when you become a free thinker, when you can forgive yourself and allow the love of that Omnipresent Essence to become a part of you. That is what individualizes you.

That's how it's been for me. And from my observations of other people, that's how it is for them. But they are blooming in their own lives, in their own ways. And it is a wonderful fragrance.

The Color Has Changed In My Life

MISS JOY: Hello, Scribe with the smiling eyes, and the same smile. How has my life bloomed? I went to a Dialogue not knowing anyone there. One of the things I recall the most was how alone I felt when I walked in. When I walked out I knew I'd never be alone again. In that first Dialogue I was told I would make a move, and where I would be moving there would be an eastern window, and to plant a flower and when it bloomed to bless it. That would be the herald that my life would change, that would be my gift from Ramtha.

About three a.m. that morning I wondered to myself, *When would I move and where would it be, how would I know it, and who all would be going with me, would that mean that I am splitting my family?* All of those thoughts kept coming in my mind. The next day I came about and put that together a little differently. I thought, *Well, let's go out and see what kind of a flower you can find and maybe plant it here.* I do have one eastern window here.

I looked high and low for the appropriate bulbs, ones that I felt a great identity with, but nothing could be found at that time of year that had a lavender hue. I happened to notice, at the last place, that down in front of the cash register were four little packages of orchids that could be planted inside or outside. But they were of a definite pink hue. I thought, *Oh, well,* so I grabbed one.

I planted that bulb to await its blossom. At the same time I did happen to have one plant in my room, a Christmas cactus of a definite pink hue also. But it was a very small plant and it hadn't bloomed for a long time. Within a week after I had planted that bulb I noticed that the plant which was originally within my home, the Christmas cactus, the one that hadn't bloomed for a long time, had a bud on it. And the bloom was certainly not pink; it was deeper than I had ever seen it before. And when it finally came out and bloomed in all of its beauty, even though the beauty was different than I had expected, I knew then that I didn't have to go out and look all over the place, the beauty was right here!

All the wisdoms of old were being presented to me through example to remind myself of what I knew. You start from Now—you start from how you are, where you are now. You begin with what is there and what you have, the talents that you have, and that's how you bloom. That little small plant with a single bloom was my greatest teacher.

A month later the *pink* hued orchids came up and blossomed in the deepest purple I had ever seen. There were four, and each one threw about twelve to fifteen blossoms. They were the most delicate, fragile blossoms I had ever seen. Those blossoms became fragile in my being, the tears streamed.

I feel that everything is *so*, and it is *me*. And I feel that that tender, fragile blossom has become what I recognize within my being. I have no words to say the feelings in my heart.

DOUGLAS: Yes you do. You just said it—*that tender, fragile blossom has become what you recognize within your being.* If you are able to recognize it, then you have become it.

MISS JOY: Ah . . . yes. The color has changed from the pink to the lavender. My attitude has changed from dismal to joy. The color has changed in the depths of my being.

IS IT NOT WONDERFUL THAT IN A SPLENDID MOMENT SORROW CAN BE RETURNED TO A SMILE

THIRTY FATHOMS, SIR

*I am Ramtha, The Enlightened
One, indeed, that which is termed
servant unto what is called the
Source, to that which is termed
the Principle Cause, indeed, unto
that which is termed Life, unto
what is called Christus—God
experiencing that which is
termed Man, Man experiencing
that which is termed God—am I
a servant unto also. And who be
He that be divine enough to be
that which is termed the tran-
quility of all things within His
being? You!*

You Have Put Yourself In Bars

RAMTHA Beloved audience that is gathered here, you are
wondrous creatures of great primal creative cause. All that
is being taught to you is being given unto you to increase
the measure of your awareness, to increase the measure of
that which is termed your knowingness, to provide you and
to allow you to be that which is termed the sovereign
entities that all of you earnestly are.

Enough of this enslavement, it is all Self-proclaimed. You
have put yourself in bars behind situations that are
difficult and arduous for you because you have created
them that way, and you suffer and you cry forth and you
seek every teacher in the land for help. But what have they
done? Well, you're still there. It is earnestly for you to
know that you who create the situations can also create the
passages out. That I teach you how to know, to allow that
which is termed the knowingness to be understood within

your being, that you can also create a utopia for yourselves rather than continuous predicaments that do not make life very amiable or desirable to be in.

Extravaganza of being is this life. In this audience this day we are going to *hold in audience*—we are going to answer the questions, but the basis of all of the answers is going to be that which is termed release and to let go of those things that bar you from being happy. What good are they? They do not allow or add to your being, they continuously take from it. This day in audience all things will be answered, but the greatest answer is going to be freedom.

In this your spring to come, all you wonderful entities that are here are going to have the first spring in your life of freedom, and the freedom is going to humble you a bit. It is going to allow you to be a bit more nimble, free and happy, but also without a lot of other things that have caused you to be quite the opposite. This is the freedom of hope, it is the Spring of Hope. And to all who are sitting in upon this audience, so shall be the answer for all of you and it shall manifest.

And what happens in freedom? Assessment. Assessment of that which is termed a new ideal, a new opportunity, a new direction, a new expression. It is a time to become. This spring all of you in this wondrous audience will have the opportunity to become the change you have always desired to occur. Only by removing the obstacles do we allow the winds of freedom to come forth. And all that are here shall be participants in it.

Why Worship You This Terrible Enslaver?

Now, one other thing here—I have moved at my own pace in your life, yes. But I have determined in each of you the right moment to allow certain things to occur, for this you have asked me to do. Time? It is an abominable enslaver. It is your greatest enigma you non-believers believe in, and you can't even see a moment or an hour yet you believe in everything that can be seen. Well, that is an unseen enslaver. Time is not dealt with in the Ongoing-Isness for there is no such thing. Time only elocates you into your hour of death; it ages your beauteous being; it oppresses, depresses and causes neuroses in you. Why worship you this terrible enslaver?

Now, I do not give credence to it. I give credence to *seasons.* Indeed everything has its season and that which is called change. But when I work with you and move with you, I do not move with you on your time and never will I. But I will move on you when the Soul is its tenderest, when it is ready for the experience. Then it comes to birth. And if it be a hundred years from this moment, it will still be; or a day or another moment, or another year, it will occur. You are so impatient—you rush yourselves into old age and then when you are old you wish you were young again [saying], "If only the days would be longer."

Well, start living by *feelings,* not times. When you do that, everything that you have ever wanted shall come forth and be born within the spectrum of your grasp if you allow it. This audience prone to impatienceness, you are going to learn how to be patient, and in that you will learn to be exceedingly glad for me, for in that I have elongated your life. And when you are still waiting, the *now* will stretch ever so long and you will have aged not one moment, and your impatienceness will turn to patient virtue and you will be happy for it. A most clever teaching indeed.

For The Jolly Goodness Of Each Of Your Beings

Now, all things are kept in the *science of keeping*— whatever is spoken, it manifests always for the glory of God, who else? For who else are *you* but the Highest of all High, and in that all things come to pass for the jolly goodness of each of your beings. Now, this freedom that we are going to bring to pass is keeping with that which is termed the prophecy that continues in the Herald of Peace that brings in your new age. This freedom will exalt you. It will exalt you in allowing you to move—to *be*.

I would rather have the lot of you have only a little bread and a little wine and a frock coat over your beings and the wilderness as your home. If, in every thought, you found peace and beauty and love and could feel not wretched about any one thing, then you would know what the kingdom of the paradise within man is all about; not this wretched groveling for all the things that you grovel for, they are very disappointing I assure you. I would have you experience freedom so that you know what it is, and all of you are going to.

We are going to remove your greatest burdens from your beings. Contemplate in the days to come what your greatest burden is, it will be removed from you; that burden will be there no more and that its space that it has created will create a vacuum; the vacuum will pull forth a great becoming, a great source for all of you—it is the gift of the wind, indeed.

Scrolls Of Questions

Now, let us begin this audience. We have great questions, scrolls of them, hearts that are wishing and wanting and we shall get on with it. So be it.

[Ramtha claps twice] Come forth indeed, wondrous *love* of my being. Open forth, as it were indeed, that all be known and all be seen. Come forth beauty in each character, dance within my Soul. And the music we create, this wondrous audience be listened upon the ears of all eternity to come. So be it. Manifested word, manifested God, come forth. So be it. Now, let us begin.

I Want A Hug And More!

RAMTHA   Traveler. You, who have lost my audience and have sought in the streets of iniquity that which is termed another entity to bring unto you that which is termed peace, what say you who return unto the land?

MASTER   I want a hug!

RAMTHA   You are a good son. Now, you see, you have lived through it *all*. Now we begin to live, Entity, happily.

MASTER   I'm ready.

RAMTHA   So you are. We shall send the runner and make you a place available for you. So be it.

MASTER   So be it. I *love* you!

RAMTHA   I am worth loving. And aye, indeed you, for you are worth it also, Entity.

MASTER   I'm worth it!

RAMTHA   Wherever I go, Entity, you are in my being, and wherever you go my word will be with you no matter who you are with or what you do. Remember that. So be it.

[Ramtha receives a lengthy kiss. The audience chuckles in surprise]

RAMTHA   One day you shall see my wondrous face, and perhaps you will contemplate whether you wish to do that again.

[Laughter]

Only Females Understand This

RAMTHA Lass, be you happy with your wondrously beautiful Self?

MASTER Yes, in one way.

RAMTHA Then you are living a duality.

MASTER No—you asked, "Am I happy with my wondrous Self?"

RAMTHA ". . . beautiful, wondrous Self."

MASTER Most of it. I'm wondrous too, aren't we all?

RAMTHA We all are indeed. You know, an artist, when he makes a wonderful painting that is beautiful, he does not enhance the beauty. He is only letting it shine through, it is already there; it has already been there all this time. Your artist had a beautiful thing to paint. [The reference is to her recent facial cosmetic surgery] Tell me, Lass, what be you that be unhappy with your wondrously beautiful Self that is so perfect?

MASTER Trivia . . . trivia.

RAMTHA Trivia? What is a *trivia*?

MASTER Something of absolutely no . . . I mean something that only entails vanity.

RAMTHA It is still an *Isness*, is it not?

MASTER It is an *Isness*.

RAMTHA Let us hear your Isness.

MASTER I don't know if you can understand this or not—only females understand this.

RAMTHA I will certainly put all of my effort into hearing it.

MASTER   Women are very particular about their hair,
their locks. If their locks look good, a woman
looks good. I had my hair cut by a hair stylist
who's supposed to be extremely good. And in
our money it was eighty-five dollars worth, and
I came away looking like I've been literally
chopped and I'm unhappy with that. I like
everything else except the hair, the hairdo he
gave me.

RAMTHA   What would you like for me to do?

MASTER   There is not much you can do about it at all. I'll
just have to become used to it.

RAMTHA   How would you like your tresses to be?

MASTER   Like they were before, before the scissors
snipped.

RAMTHA   But they covered your face up.

MASTER   That's true.

RAMTHA   But you should not cover it up any longer, it is
well worth looking at, you have a beautiful face.
Many wear their hair close to their face like a
veil to hide it. You have hid it for so long
you've become very used to it that way. It is
time to pull it back and do whatever you do [to]
let your face shine; let it be different, don't try
to hide it again. What is the use in doing this
[cosmetic surgery] if you are only going to cover
it up, aye?

Your face is quite beautiful. Have something
electrically done with your hair that allows it to
be—let me see—here, her hair is very beautiful
but, you see, you can see [her] face. You used to
cover up [your face]; you allowed your tresses to
do that. Do not do that any longer. You are
worth showing off.

191

MASTER   Otherwise, I'm quite happy.

RAMTHA   If that is the only thing that is keeping you from being happy, by all means, go and do this *straightaway*.

MASTER   Well, I mean, like I said, it's trivia. You asked me, "Did I feel good?" and I said, "I was feeling unpleasant about it." That's all. It was just a very minor thing that was bothering me and you asked and I wanted to be honest.

RAMTHA   I did do that and by all means do. So be it. Master, you are going to become more and more and more [than] you have ever dreamt of becoming. First, in being happy with Self allows all that to occur. Do this straightaway, aye?

MASTER   Okay.

RAMTHA   Women!?

Women—They Are The Birth Of Life

RAMTHA   Woman. Beautiful entity. What say you?

MASTER   I was just wondering about twins, having twins.

RAMTHA   Two knowings? [Laughter] If that which is termed twins hath been desired for you, the desire, Entity, should be put forth before that which is termed conception. If that which is termed both lives are to be within your life, feel, Entity, [that they] can learn that they can come through simultaneously. But if it is not put forth, Entity, it will not become.

You know—woman, a wondrous thing about women—I always wondered why they were thought; they were built differently, as it were indeed, their hair was always different, and

their face was always different. I began to
understand when I saw life emerge from one,
Entity, and I saw that the newborn, with the
tenderest of skin and the gentlest of its little
bones, needed something soft to lie against and
to hold it. And tresses can be put over a babe
when nursing, and tresses will keep out the
most wonderful cold there is and the babe will
stay warm.

Women, they are the birth of life. And when
they are heavy with the fruit within their
womb, Entity, they are wonders to behold for
they are giving forth a deep mystery that no
one on this plane at this time can truly explain.
There are many who do not do this, who have
done it perhaps many times before. But there
are those who do not for they are fearful of
ruining that which is termed their body. They
will *never* ruin their body. How can you ruin
your body when you give birth to yet more life?
It only compliments the body.

Beautiful woman, blessed be you and your
wondrous child and that which you bring forth
upon this plane, for all who bring forth from
their wombs this time forward bring forth
masters. They are Gods that will herald in the
new age for they are the livers of the new age,
they are advanced entities of higher cause. And
that which you carry in your beloved womb,
Entity, be not a primitive; it be a wondrous
master already understood. *All* like you will
bring forth great fruit that will bring forth an
age called the Age of Spirit, [the] Age of Light,
on this plane. That is very good. Love what you
are and cherish it. It is beautiful, Entity, and
you are blessed in your being for doing so. So
be it.

Sitting With Self

RAMTHA Master, I'm pleased you have returned to me.

MASTER I'm ecstatic with pleasure to be here with you.

RAMTHA Oh, do be that way, it is good for the being.

MASTER I was very touched . . . I *am* very touched by your comments about the spring and about, thus, myself perhaps being in a void which I am in right now, and the changes that will take place and I know they will take place, for me through trust, me having trust. Since I've seen you last I've let go of the work I've been doing in my life for the past fifteen years and for the most part right now I'm sitting.

RAMTHA Good.

MASTER I'm not working.

RAMTHA Good.

MASTER And there are highs of good feeling and lows of feeling and I'm learning to send myself love even when I'm down and that's a thrilling feeling.

RAMTHA There are a few others I could have you teach that to also.

MASTER Yes. I had questions concerning my direction—where I'm going and what will come out of all of this—and suddenly that question doesn't seem important.

RAMTHA It is important, but it will only be importantly realized when you have arrived there, in being. Allow you to get there. Just *be*, Entity.

MASTER   I feel I'm just beginning my education in knowing that inside.

RAMTHA   I am pleased.

Time Grounds The Eagles

MASTER   I have very little interest in knowing physically who I have been in the past, in my body. I have watched my mother live in the past and be a very unhappy person for it. I made a determination early in life that the past, in a negative way, is not useful in your life.

RAMTHA   The past, in *any* way, is not useful—it already has the residue of wisdom within your soul; *that* you take within you to the now. If you always look back there, you never have a future.

MASTER   And I more and more realize that the past, present and future of every moment is right now. And I have a curiosity, about the thread that has perhaps woven its way through my life all my lifetimes and exists now in the moment and perhaps continues in the future . . . my life will continue in the future.

RAMTHA   That is a certainty.

MASTER   Yes, what I would like to know is, as you know me, of that thread that winds its way eternally, what do you see that perhaps I can use on a positive level to move myself along in my own development? And, perhaps, what do you see that has been in the way that I can remove?

RAMTHA   The only thing that was ever in the way was *time*. The needing for Self-love has always been imminent. For many men throughout history, Self-love was something that they denied

themselves. [Many men throughout history]
became or purported to become that which is
termed the image of their collective societies or,
as history would have it, [became the image of]
their times. The *time*—that is a relevant thing
here that we are talking about that has *always*
stood in the way. Contemplate it—so often you
never had enough *time* to love yourself or
enough *time* to express that love or do the
things you wanted to do because you were
barred from doing them for having to do the
things you had to do.

That is not Self-*love*, Entity—that is despise of
Self and unfairness to Self by forcing Self to do
the things that are mundane, uncreative and
boring. That is more destructive to mankind,
Entity, than any threat of war is. Entities die
every day and perish, virtually of boredom.
They suffer neuroses—no ideal, no desire to live
for they mean nothing. You see, that is the
thread—when you remove time and exalt Self-
love. *Self*-love—*love* of Self—arising before
anyone and watching the spectacular dawn, aye,
and being a part of it; dancing on the rays of
the enchantress when she's allowing you to see
her full beauty. That is *Self*-love. That brings
forth unquenchable knowledge, Entity, that
allows an entity to soar to his Godhood. When
you remove those things, then you have found
your Self; that is all you ever needed to do.

Learn to create the path of happiness—learn to
create it by *living* it. That means doing what
you want to do and never, Master, do anything
that you do not want to do—ever. Ever! When
you create the path of happiness, your light

begins to emanate and virtually shall glow from
your being, for in a state of tranquil happiness
and joy, one is lifted in his being. That is all.

MASTER   Thank you.

RAMTHA   I'm pleased you are in my audience. You are
wondrously sincere, Master, and you are a noble
entity who hath the courage to do what you
have done. Most tremble and fear at that. I will
exalt you for your courage. So be it. I send you
a happy runner, an elf in nature—enjoy. So be
it.

You Will Have Your Happiness

RAMTHA   Master, what say you?

MASTER   Two . . . two questions.

RAMTHA   Ask me the second.

MASTER   Okay. The relationship that I have put aside
. . . I know it has to be put aside. It was very
rewarding for me but it was very hard to put it
aside. I'm not even sure I've put it aside.

RAMTHA   Neither am I. What desire *you*.

MASTER   Happiness.

RAMTHA   So be it. I will send you another entity. The
entity, Entity, will bring you happiness for he
will be a pool of it. This entity will help you to
understand what you are doing, for how know
you that there is anything greater if you have
nothing to compare to what you are laying
down. I will send you a comparison that makes
your choice easier. Infinitely, Master, you do
not have to choose anything if you will not to.
If this be as important unto you, Entity, let us

give an evening here, let us have you see what
would be and can be. And if what can be is not
as illustrious as what was be, we will deliver
back up what you felt you have lost and make a
greater [union] of it. That is all. Now your first.

MASTER   Is it possible for a person to be possessed by
lesser entities, and if so, have I been? And,
what I have gone through in the last week, is
that a reality or is that a fantasy?

RAMTHA   What is the reality other than life?

MASTER   It has been very fearful to me what I have been
going through.

RAMTHA   That is because you have created it. Only *you*
can create terror. Only *you* can create fear; none
can create it and give it to you lest you accept
it as such.

MASTER   I, I doubt the people that I have trusted. And I
doubt the people that I am relying on, and I
feel entrapped and I feel that I am not taking
responsibility for . . . if there is a path, I would
like to follow and I am unable to see the way
clearly to do this.

RAMTHA   Do *not* follow any path. That means it has
already been made by someone else. *Lead* your
own self, Entity, by doing what you wish to do
and create your *own* path. Do not follow
anything else. I will tell you this without your
perplexity—I have seen your perplexity and
understand it, Entity—the greatest trauma you
are suffering is that which is termed aloneness
and that which is termed guilt; that [has]
caused you to think you are being possessed by
lesser entities. There is nothing *lesser* than you.

And there is *nothing* greater than you. And you be not lesser or greater than anyone else.

But I will tell you, Entity, you cannot be possessed by anything—no thing, unseen or seen—lest you desire to be possessed, and only then [do you] taketh the semblance of attitude as a result of the entity you are wishing to be possessed by. We can *not* be possessed by anything outside of our own beings. We allow that which is termed the traumas called fear to allude into our being and to create in our being a lessening; the lessening creates that which is termed a fear called aloneness which creates in the ultimate of its being a state that is called madness.

But what causes madness is not other entities, Entity. Madness is created with the inability to cope with one's Self and all that it is creating, knowing full well it can stop anytime it wishes to. It is an escape but only into another consciousness. You never escape from anything.

If It Is Invisible, It Is A Higher Frequency

Let me set you straight. Do you think that anything that cannot be seen, that be in the Spirit nature, also has the power to possess you for you can be seen but you cannot see it? In nature, everyone fears what they cannot see, but [what] they do not realize is that anything that is unseen is closer to the Godhead than things that *can* be seen. Thus, anything of an unseen nature is more pure in its being than that which can be seen on this plane, for if it is invisible it is a higher frequency.

Woman, the madness you are creating is in your *own* being. You have asked me in the final result of your second question first, for happiness. I will see that you get it, Entity, but you must allow yourself the *receivership* of it. Permit yourself the opportunity to do so. Stop creating for yourself, lest you desire to all the abominable things that you think you are entitled to having, for feelings of remorse and guilt are putting away a good thing. That is what it is.

There are plenty of good things on this plane. *All* things are good. *Everyone* is good. And do not think yourself so least to think that there [has] been only one person that could have ever loved you or permitted you to be. For if you think that way then you have considered yourself a lesser instead of an equality here. There is a whole *universe* of entities, Master, that would delight in your personages, that would delight in that which is termed the enigma called you, your beauty, all that you are. There are even some that would permit you to be into the depths of guilt and still love you regardless.

There is more awaiting, Entity, just as there was more when you found the good that you think now that you are in trepidation for leaving behind. You never lose anything that ever belonged to you. That is a truth. When you are one hundred years old, you go and look for that which is termed the good; you will find it. You will have your happiness, Lady. Do not suffer the pains of your being with guilt and fear, remorse, any longer. Let it be enough—enough. *So be it.*

MASTER [Weeping]

RAMTHA Know you are loved? Indeed! I am a *good.* I love you, Entity, however you express, even in your madness.

MASTER [Laughing]

RAMTHA Be at peace with yourself. I will send you some runners, and some flowers. So be it. Be at peace and *learn* this day and bless the Father within you, the beauty within you, for allowing you to learn and to be. So be it.

[A pause]

You are feeling better? Is it not wonderful that in a splendid moment, Entity, sorrow can be returned to a smile. So be it.

MASTER [Smiling]

What's The Difference Between Patience And Waiting?

RAMTHA Copper-haired beauty, indeed.

MASTER How are you?

RAMTHA I am always well. Is there any other way?

MASTER No.

RAMTHA Really, you should never ask, *how are you* to anyone for they will never tell you that they are quite happy, you know. They will always look for a reason to say they are not; too simple to say that they are well and good. What desire you?

MASTER What's the difference between patience and waiting?

RAMTHA *Waiting* is intentional intent of expectancy; *patience* is being. What are you waiting for?

MASTER Well, I'm not; I'm out doing rather than waiting.

RAMTHA Lass, now, waiting means that you are expecting. That is an intent. Patience is merely being. *Being*—be what you ordinarily are, continue with it. If you are aggressive and a doer, do it. Patience does not mean, Entity, that you are sitting there waiting for the world to turn over on its side and burp. It means when you are patient that you are in a *state* of being.

Your state of being will be different than anyone else's state of being for then you are without pressure, you are without demand and you are allowed to create. That is the difference. *Being* is the most magical thing anyone can do for their illustrious Self. For then they remove all the *have to's* and *can'ts* and get down to living how they really are. It is an art.

MASTER I'm learning.

RAMTHA Well, your learning took you awhile to learn to, and, in a state of being, to become a doer.

MASTER Yes, that's true.

RAMTHA Patience, Master.

Ever Wondered What Holds The Sun Up?

MASTER In listening to the Story of Creation, I wondered who created the Sun?

RAMTHA The sun is a composite of light: the sun is from the core of God. The light is actually fed by the space or the void or that which is termed thought. You can not see [thought], but it is so powerful it can hold a great sun up. Ever

wondered what holds the sun up? It is that
which is termed space: it is the cosmic glue of
love through thought. The thoughts
continuously come and alter themselves at a
combustible point and that is what creates the
sun, Entity. It is never-ending thought bursting
into that which is termed light.

We have a kinship with the sun for the first
embodiments of our bodies is light. In bringing
forth that which is termed a Round of Creation
or creating that which is called the modular
mass, it was very necessary in order to have a
source that the mass could come from. In the
natural order of things, light is born of thought.
Thought is the eminent all Isness of all that is.
Light is its second principle. In order to give
birth to mass we must first have light, and we
must have enough of it that the light can bring
forth and concentrate and lower its Self that it
can produce the mass.

The mass will be born, not in a circular
spherical object as you would see the planets,
but it is born in a glob of mass. The mass then
sets into orbit, Entity, and the spinning
direction of the orbit creates that which is
called the spherical roundness of that which is
termed your future planet. But all thought
comes together at a central focal point. The sun
bursts forth with that blooming of that
thought. And it is ever endless.

Continuously Fed From Forever

Now, of all one hundred universes that are in
orbit, all universes surround the greatest
central source of light there is. You are actually

in orbit, in a circular orbit around a greater sun.
Contemplate for a moment that each of that
which is termed your planets that circular the
sun represent galaxies like the one that you are
in. Each planet represents a galaxy and there
are one hundred of those galaxies in orbit
around a massive light. That light, Entity, is
where all energy comes forth to alight and to
give birth to even the lower energies of your
own Mother-sun. That Principle is the simplest
working concept there ever has been and ever
will be, and it is continuously fed from
foreverness or from that which is termed
thought.

To break thought into mass you must lower it.
And the lowering of its energy shall turn
[thought into] light, and the light of its energy
shall turn to a thicker hue of blue and from blue
into gross matter and from gross matter into
the object. That is the way all things work.
Now, your Mother-sun [is a] great source of
Isness but the core, Entity, is *pure* thought.

NEWS FOR SCIENTISTS—The Sun Is Not Hot!

The creation, as it were indeed, of your earth
did not come from the cradle orbit of the sun
but was again created through the Gods and
their visualization of it. When the Babe was
created it symbolized and looked, if you had a
view of it, as a child within a womb, for your
earth, being very tiny, was surrounded in its
stratosphere—all of your oceans, all of your
waters was once what is called the Plane of
Stratum which engulfed the entirety of the
earth.

Thus, through the workings of what is called taking thought and light to yet a grosser matter, [there] had to be the matter to create its own temperature, for electrical fields create heat. In order for life to sustain upon that point of reduction it must be done with that which is termed absolute heat at the given temperature, as you term it.

Thus, the waters were put around the earth in the stratosphere. Thus, when the great sun and its light propellants reached far out into its wonderful orbit, all of the light will become reflected through that which is termed the water. Water is a conductor of light, Entity. Thus the light and warmth was evenly distributed all over your plane. There be no such things as that which is termed polar regions; all be that which is termed seventy-three degrees in your temperature understanding everywhere.

Thus, as light was diffused and softened, and heat that traveled through that which is termed the Stratum Sphere bounced back from the plane of the earth and back into the stratum, [it] created a condensation or a condensing of light, [and] called forth that which is termed heat—very simply. It does not come forth from the core of your earth outward, Entity. It is taking light and putting it together until it becomes one point that light and heat are created together.

Now, all of this time, I wish you to know, your central sun is not hot; it does *not* give off heat. It is, as it were indeed, the *totality* of light. If your scientists were right in correctly

presuming that it was gaseous heat—terrible
heat—there is no matter that has evolved
within this earth or any that set in its cradle
orbit that could withstand that amount of heat
without becoming a molten mass. That is a
truth.

Thus, the sun is not hot—it is *complete* light.
[The sun's light] propellants travel through [the
earth's] outer ridge of orbit and hit and go
through the Stratum Sphere, which is
condensed electricum, [and] bounce back off the
[earth's] surface or whatever it hits and come
back again. [That action] causes [the
propellants] to move very quickly. That is what
determines warmth, not the sun. And even the
farthest planet in your galaxy is not frigid, as
your scientists will soon learn. It has as warm a
temperature as this your earth does and is very
much inhabited.

On To Greater Adventures

MASTER   When it comes to this question of emotion and
feeling, what I have been taught is that the
emotion is connected with the solar plexus and
that the feeling is connected with the heart, and
therefore one thing that my teachers have told
me many times is that I am still too connected
with the emotion, and that adds to the
problems in my body. Yet, when you speak of
emotion and feeling I sense it as one thing.

RAMTHA   It is indeed, Lass. A thought hath no reality in
the Soul of man until it is embraced and felt,
experienced into his Soul, and recorded as
wisdom. A thought enters, Entity, through the
auric field. It comes through that which is

termed the receiver, the brain. The brain is divided in sections that qualify to various vibratory enlightenment forms called thought.

That which is termed the pituitary is the Seventh Seal, it is holy and divine. It possesses within Itself that which is termed a hormone structure that, through desire, opens itself and lets the hormones flow through the brain and to the mouth of the pineal which is the Sixth Seal, the door to the Seventh. In the flowing of these hormones, it activates another part of that which is termed the Divine Receiver, the brain, to elocate itself to accept a higher thought-frequency called *unlimitedness*. The higher thought emerges upon the brain and, in the specified area, through the door of that which is termed the Divine Seventh, fills the entire brain cavity with a different electrical frequency circuit.

The frequency is then sent through that which is termed the central nervous system. It holds forth that which is termed its mouth to receive that which is termed the electrical [projectile] that is sent through the entire system to every cellular structure within the entire body to create from thought to feeling. The entire body responds to the feeling of this electrical impulse . . . the *entire* body.

The Soul, [which] sits by that which is termed the Fourth [Seal], is called the Soul of Reckoning. The entire feeling is thus recorded within the Soul; the Soul records memory as feellngs. That is how memory is stored. If that which is termed the greater frequency hath never been felt before, the Soul, searching within itself to find audible reason for the frequency, can find none. The entity experiences a liftness within his being [that] passeth all words and all understanding, and then he equates himself as feeling greater than he has ever felt before, all because of a thought that possesses no reality until it is felt. Then the entire receiver and the entire instrument is alive with its electrical frequency, the marvel of that which is termed thought into reasoning.

Now, there is only one place that stores the frequency level of feeling; that is in the Soul. There is a cavity that sits next to the heart that no things exist in except electrical energy. Therein is where the Soul lies and has a weight content of thirteen ounces.

The Heart, 'Tis A Pump

The heart has nothing to do with feelings, only that it *responds* to the electrical impulses given to it by the Soul. Without the Soul the heart cannot stay alive, for its convulsions are derivative of that which is termed thought impulse or electrical current. The heart is a great muscle within a muscle with hollowed chambers and valves that respond electrically. It is a pump, that is all it is. It is a forever muscle that pumps the precious river of life that flows [through] the wondrous body, from the body into the lungs to gather oxygen, and to pump it throughout the body to feed the cells, that the oxygen may be obtained by the cells, that the spark of life can ignite and allow duplication to occur.

To Become Emotional Is To Become Alive

Now, emotion is the receiving of one thought and the compiling for reckoning of many [thoughts] stored already in the valuable storehouses of the Soul. To become emotional is to become alive. To become emotional creates electrical frequencies all through the entire body; [emotion] will change and lift the frequencies already available in the body according to the degree of the attitude received.

Wisdom is the product of emotion. Without emotion, one never procures the jewel called wisdom. Wisdom is an unseen knowingness experience that lies forever within the Soul that allows life's journey to be easier for that which is making the sojourn into any plane of existence. For then, any experience the entity has he will already have a record of it and does not need to do it again. Thus [the entity] gets on with greater adventures of life.

Feeling Is The Impulses From The Soul

Wisdom—it is the greatest possession that thought gives us. The emotion is the wonderfulness that we feel that does away with the intellect that is the foolish part of our beings and allows us the freedom of feeling. *Feeling* is the impulses from the Soul. That, Entity, keeps the embodiment alive. The solar plexus region is the power region. It is the Third Seal of existence. It is the amplifier of feelings, it is the Door of Power, but it has nothing to do with emotion or feelings, it only amplifies them.

The only place of storing is a Soul. It lies next to the heart in a cavity that feeds the electrical impulses into the forever muscle. Once wisdom is obtained in the Soul as memory, the feelings in turn secrete an electrical vibration back out through the auric field back into the Father to whom we owe all our beings to. That feeling that is emitted back out into the river of consciousness is gratitude and a *respond* to life.

Live In The Wonderland Of Your Dreams

Your teachers have taught you to the point that they know. The knowingness extends even greater, into a great science that is visible; it is understandable by even the stringent-minded scientists of your country and this one. This is how it works. It is infinite: it will never die, it continues on.

You are affected by emotion and feelings as all are. One who lives in his emotions rides that which is termed the seat of adventure and lives in the wonderland of dreams, a most wondrous place to be, Entity. The pain one feels from such adventure is only the change within that which is termed its magnetic electrical field surrounding its entire being. Every organ, every cell responds to its own auric vibration. If it is altered or changed in any way, the entire body responds with that change.

Your body is not depleting, you are not losing yourself; you are merely *feeling*. If the thought of fear that this has become harmful to you is introduced, indeed the thought of fear and harm will manifest in the body for a reality, just as *all* thoughts do. When one changes the attitude and accepts within his soul that everything is purpose for good, that there are *no* varying

degrees of knowledge, that there only *is;* and
when one rids one's Self of that which is termed
negativity—the balance of good and evil—and
accepts God only as *God I Am*, (there is
nothing else and yet everything is That) then
you do away with the alteredness of your being.

Thus, all thoughts that flow unto your being do
not have a positive or negative effect. They
only exalt by enhancing, expanding. Then you
never encompass pain or disease or illness, you
only exalt Self. The more the knowingness, the
lighter the embodiment becomes.

Leave The Brain To Its Own Wonderment

When the brain, through that which is termed
the Divine Seal (the pituitary) is left to its own
wonderment and allows that which is termed
unlimited creativity to flow through it, it will
activate the entire brain center which will allow
it to pick up all frequency levels. When the
body is bombarded with all of these frequency
levels of higher-graduated thought, then the
body will respond in its electrical field by being
lifted by the electrical energy—thus the body
[is] transmuting itself out of gross matter back
into light. Then you are seeing a master before
your eyes; one that has the capacity to pick up
all things and *be* it. That is how ascension is
imminent. So be it.

You are greatly loved. Do with this that I have
told you however you please, but do
contemplate it. In the midst of contemplation,
lo, Entity, you shall find that that which is
termed your divine embodiment shall grow
healthier.

Release Or Re-Lease?

MASTER   I'm going through a lot of processes right now.

RAMTHA   "Processes," a most proper word. How be my
lawgiver?

MASTER   I'm sorry, what?

RAMTHA   How be my lawgiver?

MASTER   I grabbed hold of two phrases you said earlier
at the beginning, "release" and "let go." I'm
holding onto a lot and I've given it a lot of
power, and what I'm trying to do is to take
myself to a place where I can just let go and
just release and not have to work from it
anymore. I have a lot of material things that
I'm involved in right now for some reason, and
I'm going to allow myself to ask those.

RAMTHA   Do. I desire for you to listen to me for but a
moment. What is the name of the city to which
you live in?

MASTER   Van Nuys.

RAMTHA   Do continue.

MASTER   I always have a feeling of well-being, sort of
that I'm taken care of in a way, yet there's an
underlying feeling of financial insecurity that,
even though it's not as strong, it's still there. I
can't hold onto it totally, but it still pops up in
different ways. But I get real strong feelings
that I can go ahead and do what I want and get
what I want, like I just have an abundance of
wealth but yet it hasn't manifested itself. It
appears that I'm compulsive, a compulsive
spender.

RAMTHA So no matter how much you have it will never be enough?

MASTER Yes. But yet, I do feel that there is a limit. I have put limits, and it isn't that much that I need, that I require anymore.

RAMTHA Why is that, Lass?

MASTER Because the rest of it is insignificant.

RAMTHA Why be it insignificant?

MASTER It doesn't have any meaning for me anymore; certain things that lost their importance.

RAMTHA Do you know why?

MASTER I have a feeling, it would be hard for me to put it in words, there's a feeling that is tied in with that.

RAMTHA You are absolutely correct. That is the only reason that you purchase anything, for the effect it gives you. You wanted them for so long that you visualized them and already received the effect. It doesn't matter anymore whether you get them or not.

MASTER You stated that the first time I came; I remember that and I heard that and that's true.

RAMTHA Good.

MASTER There's one thing I've held on to for so long and I'm in real search of releasing; that is the excess weight I've carried around for so many years. That is what brought me into the process I'm working on now, trying to release this and let go of it and I really have a lot of trouble in that area.

RAMTHA Why do you have the trouble?

MASTER   I'm holding on to something and I feel I can't
. . . I feel that the release is coming but I've
given it so much power and it's got so much
energy.

RAMTHA   That is a feeble excuse. How about food?

MASTER   Oh, *definitely*. That is another area I am
definitely compulsive in. I feel there's a
compulsiveness there that I *have* to deal with.
That's what I do, I feed the compulsiveness; I
feel like I'm feeding a starving person.

RAMTHA   In many ways, Master, you have been. I would
suggest that you do not cease until you are
filled and that will come even this year in your
time.

**One Of The Last Pleasures Allotted To Man
Freely**

The love of food is one of the last pleasures
allotted to man freely, and even that is
becoming an endangered act, for the ideal of
wishing to be loved by the populace and the
masses requires that you look like a starved,
poor thing that has had things done to it
unnaturally [so] that its bones protrude; and
then to bring forth the rosiness of its cheeks
you apply color so it looks healthy. Man will
become very neurotic over losing his ability to
enjoy the pleasure of consumption. He will
become so neurotic, Entity, that he will be a
miserable, unhappy entity that has to starve
himself to be accepted by an unfeeling populace.

That is not being kind to your Self or your
Being, Entity. When you truly love your
beauteous Self, when you *truly* love yourself

(the compulsiveness in what you are feeding), one day you will be able to sustain yourself without a great deal of intake and still manage to enjoy and love what you are.

I do not wish for you to lose any of this; that will not make you happy, that will take away one pleasure that you do indulge in that gratifies the entire being—the *entire* being. For if you became anything other than what you are, you would suffer a great neurosis; you would despise yourself because of the hunger that you feel and yet gravitate to proceed to indulge within the pleasures of taste and then, only when your belly is full, go and look at yourself and hate yourself for it, for a very natural act.

War With Self Only Causes War

Continue to be compulsive with your eating, and learn to look at yourself and love yourself and love and bless the food that you take into your body—rather than despising it, *love* it. When you've loved it enough, Entity, then you will learn to do it only in the measures to which you really need. That is the only way you ever conquer this sort of thing; love it into submission, you never fight it. War with Self only causes war later on, and more war, and great neurosis and unhappiness. Pleasure should not be taken from man in how he should feed himself. There is a very powerful thing—there are many religions based around what you *should* and *shouldn't*, and as long as you obey those laws you are within the accepted degree [decree] of some idiotic deity.

Eat what you want to eat—bless yourself, allow

yourself the pleasure; you will atone yourself
naturally. Food once for mankind was a
necessity—to propagate his cells, to give
strength to his embodiment, to endure his
environment. Now it has become a wonderful
art and it is much too good to pass up a niblet
of it. That is being good to yourself. Continue
to do that; you will atone naturally as I have
just spoken. Taking it away is only going to
hurt you.

That you go and deal with. You are going to
have the ferociousness of society on one side
and you are going to have the eternalness of
love on the other. You've got to choose between
which you wish to have your allegiance to. Do
you understand? That is better. In all of my
audiences I've seen brave, starving people, but
they have not been very happy. They lust for
things secretly in their soul.

The compulsiveness in regard to finance; that
will be held for a little while only to gain a little
bit more strength and direction within your
being. Let us go on to the next.

MASTER Oh, there's so much! Career . . .

RAMTHA Labor.

MASTER Yes. I have found direction and I'm headed
there and it's . . . I guess I still have to face
worthiness—something in me that's fighting
whether I'm worthy to do this, to be of service.

RAMTHA Do you want to be worthy?

MASTER Yes.

RAMTHA Then by all means, grasp it. It is a good door.
It does not mean that you are going to be

married with it and committed to it forever. It
means that it will allow you an experience, an
adventure. Go on the adventure, it will be good
for you. This place that you live, I would like to
arrange for the adventure to take you from this
place. I will see about doing that. So be it.

MASTER Thank you.

RAMTHA More?

MASTER Just a lot of feelings. I couldn't put them in
words right now.

RAMTHA Sit and feel. I will enjoy and revel in it. So be it.

MASTER Thank you.

RAMTHA Lawgiver—dispenser of Self-law.

The Morning Is Only Morning If You Declare It Is

MASTER I was raised in a way that we weren't supposed
to express our feelings.

RAMTHA Of course, they were dangerous.

MASTER But that makes it very hard to really feel. If I
had something that might be painful, I tend to
just block it out. And I don't suppose that's
good?

RAMTHA Why isn't it?

MASTER Well, you don't face what is.

RAMTHA *What is* is only if you face it; the morning is
only morning if you declare it is. In someone
else's reality, it could be night. The point is
everything is, and that *you* are the director of
your kingdom. If you do not wish to look at any
one thing, do not look at it, do not give

217

credence to it—it will become a no thing.
Unfortunately, it never has become a no thing
for you contemplate it from time to time,
certainly.

MASTER Well, how long does this go on?

RAMTHA As long as you wish for it to. You know,
Master, things can end in a moment. Just as
any one thing is contemplated in the beginning
or an upspurt, it can end in a moment only by
desiring it forth. Then the wisdom will turn into
residue within the Soul and will lie there for all
ages to come. Enough—finish it, go onto
another.

**The Only Damage You Ever Did Was To
Yourself**

Now, there we have little lingerings of guilt
which is an untended business, fear which is an
untended business, insecurity and
unworthiness—all of those things are very
powerful emotions that help constitute and
make up the collective attitude to which you
express so eloquently. Then you must say,
"Alas, do I wish to fear anything? No, bring
forth all my fear." Then we have what is called
the Days of Reckoning and a *fire*, doubt and all
of that. But it is usually finished. Of guilt, we
bring up all guilt and you see the folly of it. The
only damage you ever did, Entity, was to
yourself by allowing you to feel that way—kept
you from having a jolly good time. You
understand?

MASTER Will this weekend bring a healing to my family?

RAMTHA It will indeed, Master, if the only thing that
you do is love them in spite of themselves; for if

you set the light premise it will allow them
greater ease in expressing around you. What is
more important than to love? It is a much
[more] soothing, simpler, elocating feeling upon
your being than the trepidations of fear and
guilt and insecurity. Love them enough to allow
them to be. That is all you have to do. Love
yourself enough to allow your Self to be, in
spite of everything else.

Master, of feelings; a *master* of feelings
understands all feelings but he desires after
that which is termed the grandest of feelings,
and that is love, for everything comes forth
from that measure. Just be—*be.* Look at each of
their faces and see [your Self]. So *be* it. What
more can a teacher do but to instill knowledge,
and [the premise of] being happy about having
that knowledge. You know, you have done a
great thing. I am pleased, Entity. So be it. Go
and enjoy.

Tired Of Being A Chimney

MASTER Well, I feel pretty okay. I want to fall in love,
that's all I want.

RAMTHA So *be* it; you will.

MASTER Soon?

RAMTHA Stipulations to love?

MASTER I also want to stop smoking and I'd like some
help so that it's an easy thing, so that it's not
so difficult. I've done it before but I never felt I
was a non-smoker. I really want to stop
smoking and I'd really like some help.

RAMTHA I will help you but you must help yourself. You

219

are not an invalid, Entity. You, who have
directed the habit, can also misdirect it and
cease it.

MASTER Okay.

RAMTHA All you have to do is want to live.

MASTER Well I do, but I also want to smoke while I'm
living.

RAMTHA Then go and acquire yourself a little pipe and
puff on it; the air will do your lungs good.

MASTER That wasn't what I had in mind, but I'll try it.
Is there anything you can tell me about what I
should be doing or what I'm doing?

RAMTHA You have already desired what you want to do
and what you want to have happen. We will
just let that occur. That will be good enough.

The Promise

RAMTHA This that you are wearing upon your
breastplate, aye, be it a rainbow?

MASTER Yes.

RAMTHA Do you know why there is such a phenomenon?

MASTER No.

RAMTHA Why do you wear it if you do not know why it
is?

MASTER Because it is pretty; because I like the colors.

RAMTHA Ah. A rainbow is a promise, Entity. They only
had rainbows when the oceans came down
outside of the Plane of Terra. You have a planet
in your solar system called Venus. It is

surrounded in clouds; the clouds are really its
future oceans. Once your earth was the same
way, and the earth was able to grow and to
manifest and to propagate life through a
diffused light element that caused a moderate
temperature all over the place. When you take
and diffuse light through the conduit of water
you get an even lighting. You also get even
heating so the little child inside the womb
begins to grow.

On earth, the miracle of a rainbow never existed
until the waters fell as is recorded in your
history and is called the Great Flood. And when
the clouds rained down many who were on the
plane at that time saw the sun for the first time
through man's eyes—a great and fiery object.
And so immense and wonderful was such a
sight that it was made a great God and
worshipped in ancient temples, not only on the
land mass Lemuria and Atlatia but all through
Persia and Africa and Egypt.

When all the waters had rained down, the great
and wondrous sun lit the air that was fresh and
clean. And the wonderful light, immersed upon
that which is termed the warm moisture in the
air, created a spectrum of color. And when the
sun came forth, Master, in all of its brilliance,
the same colors that were seen in floral textures
began to take on the same magnificent color
scheme in the sky. This spectral display never
existed before.

Your rainbow, in its understanding, is a
promise: every time you see it, it is the promise
being kept that the world and all of its
occupants shall never be destroyed again. That

is the promise of the God Ra, the great sun.
Wear it and be exceedingly happy—it is the
dawning of realization. So be it.

I Saw A Phony-Baloney

MASTER   That was a marvelous story. Thank you for
being here.

RAMTHA   Well, I'm very pleased that you are here and
thanking me for all of this, Entity, but do also
give Self gratification for allowing the
experiences. There are many entities that want
and they come unceasingly, and they want,
want, *want.* Well, we give, give, *give* but most
of them do not want to receive what they are
asking for so they send it away and it is *on
hold,* as it were indeed; they become oppressed
because they do not get everything they want
when it is *they* who shut the door.

Well, you are one who does not shut the door.
You, little girl, I'm very pleased with your
progress and also with the health of the body.
So be it. Because you have learned to artfully
live in the moment, what greater teacher could
[there] be than you to teach others to live
artfully. Goals are well and good but they also
are indicative of failure. That brings many
entities to grow up into this life being very
conscious of failure. Get rid of them. Learn to
live in this now, in this moment—allow yourself
to flow.

Routines that you can set are understandable,
but never make out that which you attempt to
achieve during that routine. Simply *allow* the
days to come. And whatever will be in those
days *let* them be. You will find your whole life

changed and enriched and after all, you, who
have been seeking so much enlightenment, so
much knowledge—high and low you have been
looking for it—you will never get it or
understand what you have been looking for
until you allow yourself the life to find out
about it.

MASTER I believe what you are saying to me is not to
worry about the goal but to be involved in the
process of doing it and living it?

RAMTHA Earnestly, *earnestly*. Creativity is lost when the
value is seen first—that is the way it is.
Creativity is made immortal when the object of
creativity is lost. Your papyrus that you are
struggling with is only another creative form to
allow that which you are and know to come
forth in an expressively beautiful form. Then
you will become the benefactor of [that
beautiful form] because it will enhance you.
Then whatever it enhances thereafter, called
success, is only *after* the great thing that has
been achieved in your own life. It *will* be
successful, but please allow Self to express and
worry not of anything else.

MASTER I feel that I know the truth of what you say.
The fear caught me and the creativity of the
expression was stopped with that, and I hear
you. Thank you.

RAMTHA Master, if I told you that your greatest
happiness would be losing everything that you
had, every honor, every award, noble house,
vehicle and all, and to move to a place far from
this place and to begin again, that your
greatest happiness will be there in fulfillment
and joy, you would not do that.

MASTER I probably wouldn't and I know it's true.

RAMTHA Now, to become enlightened is to make the priority of enlightenment first—the priority of love of Self *first*. You think you love yourself for all that you have surrounded around you and learned. But in the reality that is called *reality*, you have become encumbered to it, enslaved, and you have lost your identity and even your glow. Love of Self means to get ahold of Self again. The vehicles of understanding are right before you.

In this spring I desire for you to take stock in Self. You can be happy with everything that you do. You are a wonderful teacher—love flows through your being like a river. But you will not see that come to pass until you have made peace with your life. No teacher, no master, no whoever, is going to make any difference until you allow it to occur. So be it.

MASTER So be it.

RAMTHA I assure you, you are loved explicitly in greater understandings, and your value to this plane, Entity, you have not even the eyes to see it as of yet. But there is a purpose in your being that will come when you begin it. And forget all of the illusion that you put on outward. So be it.

MASTER Thank you for saying it enough that I heard it.

RAMTHA There is a word I have heard that I found most curious and I went to a marketplace to see if there was such a creature and, lo, I found them everywhere. It is called *phony-baloney*. I saw what a phony-baloney looked like. I understand that baloney is a meat that is put together;

actually it is remnants of better cuts that have been mashed and processed and sliced and all that. Phony-baloney is the term that the cities are full of. Everyone is so into being a phony-baloney no one knows the reality that lies behind the different illusions that are being exploited.

Now, to find a true gem of evenness, one who speaks evenly that no matter what they say you can always trust, that their word is how they are—that is a jewel. And those who learn to speak evenly and from that which is termed *complete* love of Self to the creature in front of it, they will be exalted and their Isness and their source will be rewarded many times. Entity, you are a jewel amongst women and men. Continue to speak evenly. So be it, and now we are not a phony-baloney, aye!

You Have Only Eaten A Small Portion Of It

MASTER I've been doing my pretending; I've been very happy with it. As I do my pretending I feel that I am more God than at any other time.

RAMTHA Know why?

MASTER Well, it feels nice and I'm going on the basis of feeling.

RAMTHA It's a creative image; you are creating a character. You are letting your tresses grow upon your shoulders to keep your neck warm?

MASTER There is a certain role in my pretending.

RAMTHA Ah, it is the evil character?

MASTER Indeed, especially the facial hair. It suggests an

evil character in the masked consciousness for some reason.

RAMTHA Where do you think your evilness is?

MASTER Evilness—that's a creation of . . . that is created by a God who chooses to create it. In terms of entertainments, it seems that by symbolizing evil in a human form it makes it finite and therefore contains the fears of the audience in a finite form, and therefore can be overcome. That seems to be the rationale behind it. Is there any guidance or projection you can make concerning the progress of my career?

RAMTHA You are very loved, very much, for what you do. You are considered very fine in what you portray. Your career, as you term it, will progress as has been ordained by your wish. The more that you do it the better you will become, for the more you do it the better oriented you will become toward it. Then, the perfection of your finite age will increase, thus the demand for your brilliance [will increase] also. Consider this school.

RAMTHA Are you pleased with your life and fair-haired women?

MASTER Very . . . yes, I've been learning things in this regard. And the most valuable lesson I've learned has come from experience since you spoke of the beauty of the Soul being more important than the beauty of the skin.

RAMTHA It certainly is.

MASTER I'm learning this on a subjective experience level, and the lesson has been far easier than I had imagined.

RAMTHA You are not trying to make such an impression
on the flesh, that is why it is easier. Continue to
learn, Master, and revel in love. It is good for
the Soul. So be it. You have come a long way
from the vast table I have set before you. You
have only eaten a small portion of it. There is
still a great amount to go. So be it.

The Best Thing For Both Of You Are One Another

RAMTHA Master. Indeed.

MASTER Hi. Do you think maybe you could help us with
some things that could happen here while we're
here for the month so that we could have some
greater understanding of what would be a good
place to be?

RAMTHA It should not be dependent upon what can
happen for you. That is taking the control out
of your being and giving it to the will of others.
The reason that you are here is to contemplate
Self and allow Self rest, and to see things and
the importance and priority of things wherever
you go. You and your wonderful entity will
always do very well. Of course, the extent of
that *very well* can oftentimes be unquenchable
yet, at some times, it takes very little to quench
it. That is where you are happiest the most.

That is what was desired for your journey here,
to allow you to be—to be a different
understanding, a different climate, a different
consciousness. That is all I want you to do for
the time that you are here. There [is] no
importance of making any decisions—only
being. I will help you to realize the
opportunities that are available to you. But

they should not change your mind; it should already be set within you, what is the priority of the two of you.

MASTER   That's what's important. I realize more than ever that all of my questions are me and him. That's the only thing that's important, to find the best thing for both of us.

RAMTHA   The best thing for both of you are one another.

MASTER   Oh, you're not kiddin'.

RAMTHA   And wherever you are together, the doors of opportunity will open to you. Give yourself a little moment or two to contemplate that and be happy. So be it.

In Service To Self Is Quite Enough

MASTER   My main concern is what my path of service is in my life.

RAMTHA   To you.

MASTER   To myself and my fellow man.

RAMTHA   Don't worry about your *fellow* man. If you become happy, however they look upon you doesn't make any difference. The fact that you *are* happy and in service to Self is quite enough. Now, when you become happy we will send some runners [so] that you can express your Self. But mind you, that which is termed the marketplace is a very rigorous, dangerous place in which to express infinite thoughts.

MASTER   I am looking for the best avenue for my potential and my ability, the *best* outlet for my creativity and my potential, and I would like it to be of service in some way.

RAMTHA Everything you do is of service, to *you*. Do not ever come out to serve anyone else. That is a misunderstanding, for you never will, for you will never give them enough. Serve yourself. Everything that you do is serving yourself. Honor yourself first. Find a beauty that is there *first*, Entity. Then, by being you, you can be a light to others but not their victims. We will open the avenue up. Continue to learn about you and to serve yourself, and to be kind and to learn to be calm in the tempers of others that are around you. Then at such time, Entity, we are going to make a move. We are going to take you to a land that you can express how you are. And the light of your being and the work of your being will help many. So be it.

The Spell Of A Woman

RAMTHA How feel you in this relationship now? [The question is directed at a couple]

MASTER [The male answers] I feel very good. [They look at each other and hold hands]

RAMTHA And in regard to sharing a hovel together?

MASTER [They laugh in surprise, the male responds] Ah . . . good, good. The thing that comes up . . . what comes up is, uh . . . my major difficulty is . . . ah, um . . . one's dramatics; one's, ah . . . it's only a personal thing . . . her being an actress or, her being a pretender. Uh, it's so hard to express.

RAMTHA She becomes dramatic and overemphasizes difficulties!

MASTER *Right.* It couldn't be said better. [Audience

joins in their laughter] That's just so right, and I'm more into just letting it be.

RAMTHA   Let it be.

MASTER   And what comes up is, from that end, is me not being able to confront things and I just want to let it be.

RAMTHA   My Master [who is] under the spell of a woman, it is in their natures to be often in this particular understanding for they are born strongly of emotion and it is a good thing that they are. What you must learn to master is to get used to these tantrums of emotion and do not deal with anything until they have run their course. You will learn to be a wise and noble man that will gain the respect of your woman if you will let her have her tantrums and dramatic display however frugal or however great it is. And when she is all finished intuitively you will know how to deal with it, for when she is finished it will be finished.

Don't make a decision, don't. Simply be and allow her to be. And if she gets upset (an appropriate term I have heard) and even becomes more so because you are not responding how she would be, look at her and tell her that you love her and that when she is quite finished then you'll come back and talk with her sensibly.

MASTER   Ah, that's so perfect. That's beautiful.

RAMTHA   My beloved Master, do that. No matter what you do she is going to love you—that is self-evident. In order to "put up with her," love her enough to get her to express what she needs to express. It is not going to change anything; it

is only going to make her feel better or worse or
however she chooses to feel. Continue to be and
go and be happy. Your life may get monotonous
from this but to take on the sheen of dullness it
won't.

MASTER   About my health?

RAMTHA   A little more rest. The body is fatigued and you
sometimes push it a little more than it needs.
Only be quiet and peaceful for a little bit, aye.
Go find a wondrous object and contemplate on
it. The body regenerates itself once you do that.
So be it.

MASTER   I love you very much.

RAMTHA   And I love you very much. You are a blessing
to your woman and she is a blessing to you.
Together you make my Soul very warm. Your
years together will earn the right to be together
[because of] your temperaments toward one
another. And God will display Itself beautifully
in both lives. I am very pleased with
you—never forget that.

MASTER   I never will. Thank you, thank you very much.

RAMTHA   Live in peace, or whatever the moment dictates.

Your Soul Does Not Have Any Wrinkles Upon It

MASTER   I was wondering if you could talk a little bit
about the difference between the thought and
the act. And also, what is it in man that is the
creative process, that takes care of the creative
process? Is it the Soul? And if the Soul, as you
said, measures . . .

RAMTHA   . . . thirteen ounces

MASTER . . . it must live in space and time?

RAMTHA It does indeed, but within the man; within his chest, that is where his subconscious lies.

MASTER In the beginning, you talked about time as an illusion. And if the Soul lives in time, what is it that lives out of time?

RAMTHA Foreverness, which the Soul is. The Soul cannot help but live in time for it is encased within an entity that is continuously producing itself life after life after life after life, whose ending and beginning of life is dictated by time and the illusion. Your Soul never changes its continuousness, which is called forever, that does exist outside of time. There is no time that equates forever. Time equates an ongoingness that is measured in waves, but foreverness is the now that is a continuum. The Soul is also that.

MASTER That can't be understood through the mind, can it?

RAMTHA The body can understand it if permitted to understand it by doing away with time. Seasons come and go but that does not dictate time. Seasons are in the natural order of breath like breath is to the body an expulsion, an expansion, a creativeness which goes on in every cell within your body. If you cease in that which is termed time, and start the beginning of now as forever, that this *now* is all that is important, the Soul will continuously record *now* rather than hours indicative of growing older, or birthdays that advance you into death. Live *now*, Entity, and the Soul will regulate the hormone activity within the body that allows the body to sustain itself in the equalum that is called now. That is achieved in the body.

The only reason that anyone grows old is that they're expected to. They think *old.* They have days that [are] celebrated in great hosts with all sorts of novelties—their birthday. And treacherous entities that celebrate the day you are getting older; they are hurrying you with great laughter and expediency into dying. You see, when you do away with those things—age and the concept of eternity and astrologies— you will do away with aging and dying.

Death warrants and limits the activity of the entity upon the Plane of Demonstration. You know, your Soul does not have any wrinkles upon it. Your Spirit, it often walks in front of you—brilliant Light, [it] has always been a *brilliant* Light. And the immortalness of the Soul that you have, that you could not occupy Thought unless you have it, will never change. It only equips itself more and more with the wisdom of the experience and the virtues of adventures that allow the reasoning part—the Spirit, Soul and Ego—to come together to be poignant in its decisions and attitudes.

In the beginning of the onslaught of man, even up to as close as that which is termed three thousand years ago in your time, entities were living until that which is termed their five hundredth year. Only did man become what you call limited and civilized, did his life span shorten. When the calendar was created so was the ending of the life-span of man. That is a truth. [Time is an] illusion indeed, but the most awesome one that rules this plane, for you [are] permitted to act only within the realms of time.

Is There Ever A Reason Not To Be Loving?

RAMTHA Master.

MASTER You're wonderful.

RAMTHA Indeed I am. I am pleased that you have taken stock to notice. But know why I am? Why am I wonderful?

MASTER You're so loving. I sit here and I smile.

RAMTHA Have I ever found a reason not to be loving?

MASTER No.

RAMTHA Then, what be I who cannot find a reason for not loving? What kind of creature must you become that there is no reason worth not loving? [What kind of creature] understands entities like you and everyone else and loves them? God. You can see [that] in me to be wonderful. I am. So be you if you allow yourself to master the things that inhibit you.

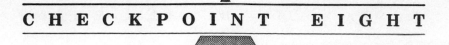
A NEW WIND
WILL BLOW
AND BEHOLD
ALL THAT MAN
DREAMS IN HIS
SOUL

THE WIND IN THE SAILS

235

God, the Father, the Magnificent,
the Fabulous, the Miraculous, the
Isness, the Totality, does not
have an ego to judge good or bad.
That was given to His beloved
Son to which all of you are, for
only you possess the will of
creativity. God, the Father, is the
mass that you create from, but
He hath created everything in a
state of joy for He is all things.

What You Are Is Happiness

RAMTHA Master, what say you.

MASTER I'm perfectly content—filled with joy, love, compassion.

RAMTHA Yes, 'tis true.

MASTER What is there to say?

RAMTHA Continue to do what brings you those thoughts today.

MASTER Indeed.

RAMTHA Our first audience, long ago in your illusion?

MASTER Yes . . . this is an anniversary, yes.

RAMTHA Indeed it is.

MASTER It's been a year.

RAMTHA You could have not conceived of all the changes. What you are is happiness, Entity. The seeds of it are going to grow now. Be glad that those things are no more, that this freedom hath come forth indeed. We bless you and we continue to exalt you. I have kept my word. So be it.

I Felt Touched By That Inside

RAMTHA Master.

MASTER I have a very deep sense, and I have for a long time, that my husband and I are Soulmates. I'm asking you if this is so. I don't even know what a Soulmate is, to tell you the truth.

RAMTHA All you want to know is if you have one.

MASTER I'll tell you what I think a Soulmate is and maybe that will be the answer. It's deeper than the surface; it's like I feel as though there's a very deep root in our relationship that goes beyond what we have in common on a superficial level, that we have a great deal in common on a *Soul* level.

RAMTHA That is correct, you are precisely correct. How feel you, Lord?

MASTER As she was talking about that I felt touched by that inside. That's the only knowing I have—in here.

RAMTHA That is all the truth you need. You have answered your question.

MASTER Thank you.

RAMTHA You never have to worry about going and looking for another.

MASTER For a long time I thought that I did and it's only been in the last few years that I realized that's not necessary.

RAMTHA So many go and question themselves, and they want so many things for themselves and it really gets in the way of understanding Self—they are deterrents in many ways though they are adventures. And other people get in the way and perhaps [they become] desirous of other peoples. But usually when you find out that the other people are not so desirable as you thought they were, and then when you get down to the business of appreciating Self does the realization finally occur. Then you are through the *fire*.

Now, you are on your path that you are creating of complete becoming. You don't have to look any more. It is not necessary. There is no need for more marriages or relationships. They are one in the same. There is only a need now to be and to relax and to become, and that will be Self-evident in the both of you. So be it. Enjoy it.

The Enoughness Called Wisdom

MASTER I wish to travel and see other places.

RAMTHA Well, you have not seen everything that is here. You always think that every place else is better. You know, Lass, you think we can get in a great airship and fly away and leave all of our problems behind? Well, that is not necessarily so. What causes difficulties and unhappinesses locked within us has nothing to do with the land mass. Do see a little bit more of what is around here. It is wonderful, terrifying and exciting. And learn to be at peace a little bit more with your life. So be it.

MASTER Well, all I want is woods and maybe a little bark to make a shelter.

RAMTHA But why? Why? I will tell you why—the non-competitiveness of consciousness; where there are no people there's bound to be purity. Without a person, who is to recognize the purity? Go and have that, then. Simply do it, there is nothing holding you back. Go and do it and find your place to do that in. And when your heart is all at peace, then everything within you is even. Then you write about your experience and share the innocence with someone else. So be it.

MASTER Are you aware of my situation right now?

RAMTHA I'm aware of your unhappiness, Master. Change it!

MASTER I'm ready to release. I think the past year everything has been amplified so I could choose.

RAMTHA That is correct.

MASTER I want to enjoy life and I want to . . . whatever it is in me that stops me I just want it gone.

RAMTHA Then go and do what you want to do where there is no one else. Then there will be no one to remind you of your choices. None. There is no God, no one, that can change your insides. There is no right for us to do that. *That* you must learn. The only way one ever conquers it is to become what his desire is until he has had enough of it. It is the enoughness called wisdom that means he never has to do it anymore—it is finished. Go and be and do.

MASTER When is the attitude enough to restore the body?

RAMTHA When there is *no* doubt that happiness exists within the being. And *that* is a feat. That is all. Go and be happy and go to your wilderness.

MASTER Is there anything else?

RAMTHA Only that you are loved. And this whole trek and journey, Entity, has been a sovereign cleansing to the Soul. So be it. Go and be happy.

Permit Dreams To Come True

MASTER I know everyone takes responsibility for being in a relationship, but maybe I shouldn't be married. Yet, the dream that always comes up for me is at the snow and is at the sea and is with children around, and is with flowers and with me cooking and my family there, and the peace of all the good things I learned from my mother, with the popcorn and the hot chocolate and it was okay if it was raining . . . so it's raining, great, let's just be together.

RAMTHA Is it a discredit to your ego to have two marriages rather than one?

MASTER Within me? No.

RAMTHA Within who?

MASTER I deal a lot with the outside, with other entities. I always have. I don't want to be jumping.

RAMTHA Why not? Is not "jumping" change and adventure and experience? All of those things [in your dream] are idealistic reality, born in a dream only because you will not permit them to occur for fear of criticism by those who may be watching.

241

MASTER Are you saying that I'm not doing these things; that I am just dreaming of them?

RAMTHA You *are* doing those things, Entity; they are to fulfill yourself—your Self, no one else. But unfortunately you think it must be with the first entity or even the second, at most, and you throw all of the responsibility of making that dream come true on them, and then you complain that you have hurt them when actually it is you who has been disappointed. That is a truth.

When you come to terms with that which is termed your ego and [come to terms with your understandings of], "Not having so many marriages or relationships"—if you lie with a man and give him your heart and love him, that is more sacred than marriage—when you allow your Self to express freely without the condemnation of those that are around you and allow your Self enough love through the experiencing [of the] wonderful adventure of other entities, until you find *that* dream you are never going to have it except in slumber.

Your pride needs to be bruised and so does your altered ego for you are trying to hold an ideal that no one holds. Even he who is married but one time has been married a hundred times. Learn to be free and express. Marriage is not indoctrination—it is an *allowing*, it is a *sharing*. There is nothing to do with law and papers; it has everything to do with the Soul and Spirit. Allow yourself to feel, to express. Allow yourself to laugh. And one day your dream will come true for you will have grown enough to allow the magnificence of all these things to

occur by being more vulnerable and less
protected.

The talk I hear, I hear. But you put too many
rigid controls on answers. And those controls, I
tell you, must also confess up to be that which
is termed the ideals of others around you. I will
not have it for I am not in that nature; I am a
grand God that sees the allness of all. And in
that allness I can see the minuteness of
limitation, and you have surrounded yourself
with it and do not permit dreams to come true
all because of your pride and your altered ego.
Though you have had two marriages, how many
relationships have you had in your life? That
equates marriage. If you have a hundred more
before your dream comes true, they will have all
been worth it for they have added to the value
of appreciation through experience. Go about
and contemplate that for awhile in your silent
aloneness.

Give Birth To Self First

You are not androgynous, Entity. You shall not
give birth to your own family and husbandman
by yourself. You are going to have to give birth
to Self, to allow all of those things outside of
your being to come to pass. And it is well and
good to be with Self for there are no dangers—
you are protected and there are no commit-
ments, that is paradise. When you are wanting
to fulfill dreams you must interact with others.
Do permit yourself the grace to do it. Don't be
so ugly upon your being. That is all.

You are greatly loved—*greatly*. Allow your Self
enough of this love to experience it whenever it
comes. Then you will understand how to live as

a God and behold what you are doing in noble virtue in the broadness of all. Society—they secretly despise you because they wish they could do it. That is how it is.

MASTER So I'm to go and contemplate this?

RAMTHA Indeed.

MASTER Alone?

RAMTHA Alone. And think how silly it is to deny one Self for the frugal thoughts of those around you. Do you want all of those dreams? They will come to pass, but only when you are allowed to share and to give and to be your Self. And when it is finished, it is finished and behold there appears another.

MASTER Thank you.

RAMTHA I am pleased that you have tolerated my listening, Entity. It is a bit good for you. So be it.

Where Is The Mercy And The Love?

MASTER Can you help me?

RAMTHA We will remove the fear by amplifying it. That is all you need.

MASTER Do I have the fear of having children or is there an experience in my past that makes me fearful about that?

RAMTHA The consciousness, Entity, makes you fearful. Contemplate this consciousness on this plane, think about it. What does it expect of children? What does it do with them? How are they taught? What happens to them? Where is the mercy and the love? How can you rear them up? Are you a good parent or a bad parent and all of that. If you contemplate that thoroughly in what is called seven days in your time, you will have all the answers and the fear will be removed. Then we can proceed. So be it.

A Do-Gooder

MASTER   I have a few considerations I would like to discuss. After my father passed, the family unit split—his mother and sisters have been against my mother. Is there something I could do to bring us all back together? No? Why is that?

RAMTHA   Who are you to bring them all together again? If you keep the love for *all* and see that this is a very small truth that they're expressing, then, very soon, they will see it also. There are many what is called *a do-gooder*. A very wondrous term indeed. But a do-gooder is an enslaver, for they think that they should go and save the world, or amend situations to which they have no business [amending] for the situations need to occur in order for a working or a desire to be fulfilled, and who are they to say what that is.

Best to love them all and don't take sides—love them and allow them to be. In the wisdom of this act you will see the workings and you will not lose favor with anyone, more importantly yourself, because of it. So be it.

I Looked Far And Wide For The Creature

MASTER   What is the devil? [asks a young person]

RAMTHA   The devil? What think you the devil to be?

MASTER   I think the devil is something in somebody's mind, that he puts so much thought into it that it became a reality to this person. And that he does believe in it and it *is* a reality but a reality to *him*, and it is in a lot of peoples' minds, and it's a thought.

RAMTHA Correct. Now, if one believes in the devil and another doesn't, who is right, who is true?

MASTER Both of them are.

RAMTHA Why?

MASTER Because each one of them has their own truth.

RAMTHA Correct, correct. Now, the devil was a masterful ploy by a conquering institution to put the fear of God, most literally, unto the hearts of little ones—that God had created a monster that would *get them* lest they be good to him. The devil was used to control the world most effectively and even today it is still feared and believed. Someone conjured it up—a God—and thus it became, but only to those who believed. That is how it is.

I will tell you, Master, you have answered very well for that is precisely [what] it is. But I wish to tell you this and let us reason this on this plane; you ascertain that God, the Principle, is all things, correct? Is He the rose? Is He the gown? Is He the light? Is He the rug? Is He the structure? What is God not, aye?

MASTER God's everything.

RAMTHA Now, if God made the Devil, then what is the Devil made out of?

MASTER God.

RAMTHA Ah, so we must conclude that the devil has good in him, aye? So the devil is really not evil,

aye, because he's really God, aye? Who else
would he be? Now, this wonderful, creative
Source, Infinite Principle is egoless. God, the
Father, the Magnificent, the Fabulous, the
Miraculous, the Isness, the Totality, does not
have an ego to judge good or bad. That was
given to His beloved Son to which all of you
are, for only you possess the will of
creativity—He is the mass that you create
from, but He hath created everything in a state
of joy for He is all things.

Thus, beloved Master, if the Father had created
the devil and the devil be a condemning entity
that despises the little ones and early mornings,
and the flight of wild fowl to the southernmost
regions, and the wind on the water, and the
changing of leaves, and the timeless eloquence
of a woman's beauty or a man's honor; if He
despises all of those things then God, the
infinite principle, despises *Himself!*

What you all fear is this Principle that is the
Wind on the Water and the great Oak Tree in
the midst of a winter night with snow hanging
heavily in its boughs. This Principle hath never
created anything that would ever take life from
anyone for He *is* everyone and everything, and
He is ongoing-totality-Isness. In knowing this,
Master, God created no devil. Only man did
that as he measured to enslave; to inflict
torment and fear on creeds of people to enslave
them. This wonderful God that I know is All
Things, and loves you for *you* are the apple of
His eye. When He looks upon you He sees
Himself, and Himself is eternity.

You Are All Beyond The Reach

No, there is no hell and there is no devil. There is only Life and a splendid Father who shall become all things to whatever His beloved Son, which you are, desires Him to become in order for His beloved Son to experience the treasure called feelings. You are perpetual, lad. You will go on and on and on. And the long, hard reach of a past buried in some remote place that created such a vile creature will never catch you, for you are in the wind beyond the reach.

Those who believe in such creatures also fear God and secretly despise Him for creating such a monster to keep them [in] torment. They are taught to fear God, not to love Him. You can never love anything you fear; you secretly despise it for it keeps you humbled.

This God [that I know] is infinite. One day all the superstitious entities that were terrified by such an awful creature will see the folly and the knowingness as to why it was really created. It is a no thing. For those who believe, that is their truth for they have created it to be so. For those to acknowledge the Source, that is the Isness. That is how it is.

Devil? I looked far and wide for the creature; into the depths of your earth to a hell that was supposed to be a burning lake and I found a hollowed sphere. No, he wasn't there. And I went into the deepest parts of your space to where the cold is beyond knowingness, and since [it is said] he a lover of "hellfire and brimstone," I didn't find him in the great cold. I looked everywhere, I found him nowhere. And I returned and lo, I found him thriving in the hearts of frenzied entities in a fervor of madness to save the world from its sins. That is where he is. You understand?

Can Any Place Capture The Morning Rods Of A Golden Sun?

God is breathtaking morning of a quiet, so quiet that the whispers of ancient places become vivid in the twinkling of the early morning stars. And a moon that has waxed and waned all night, and a morning coming vividly alive on the horizon of the east. God is the splendidness of ongoingness—He is life. Love life, love you—*you* are God.

What grand temple has been erected for his greatness, his esteemed principle, his awesome beauty? Can any place capture the morning rods of a golden sun? Or [capture] the beams of the enchantress when she is in full bloom at midnight as her children, the stars, twinkle and dance in the heavens? There is no place that has ever been made that could honor such an entity that is all things, except in you.

Love you and this life, you wondrous Creator. Then you love that which is termed the *God I Am,* the Ongoing Principle—Peace and Joy. Then you are in servants to and are the all-wise, knowing intelligence of forever. When those that are still wishing the world to end, [those] who hate everyone because they don't believe the way they believe, when you can no longer hear their echoes in the early morning and only hear a morning bird saluting the beautifulness of a risen rosy dawn, when that is all you hear,

then you are listening to the voice of God in his
ongoingness of foreverness.

Life . . . live it to the fullest. Love yourself
completely for then you love God. That is how
it is. And one day, Master, everyone will know
that, and behold, a new kingdom is born. You
are a wise master. Never forget these things
you have learned, that you may teach them by
becoming them.

The greatest sword that was ever created was
never forged of that which is termed metals; it
was forged of superstition and fear. That
conquered the world and still does. What a
folly!

Start Loving This Beauteous Place

RAMTHA Beloved Master, indeed what say you?

MASTER Beloved Master.

RAMTHA Indeed I am and so be you.

MASTER I know. Some of the sages and Edgar Cayce, to
speak of, have predicted grave disasters for the
earth. Are these going to be so?

RAMTHA Because one sage predicted it the earth is going
to crumble and be in despair of millions upon
millions? No. Who hath the power to determine
an ending to an exquisite life that is really
ongoing? No one! I will tell you, Lord, and it be
a truth, in your marketplace that which is
termed the defiling of the body sells, fear sells,
terror sells. If someone prophesied that the
world would go on and gracefully bloom itself
into another time period and would continue to

get better and better, no one would purchase such words in the marketplace.

But if someone says that the world is going to split in half and blow up and continents sink, all of these terrible things, everyone scrambles to purchase it for they all live here in a state of terror. And how ridiculous, the continents sinking; where would the ocean go? This plane's normality is not governed in love but rather in fear. That is how it is. So, in order to become well known, one predicts fear. In order to become well versed in prophesy, always prophetize doom but always do it well enough outside of your own lifetime that you are not here when it all does not happen.

You know, before that which is called the rage of your Christianity began, no one considered the ending of life. [They] only [considered] war—that was an ending of a moment but not life immortal. If it was, man would have never erected temples like the great fiery forms, or the Acropolis, or wonderful, mystic places high on forgotten mountains. You would have never erected that for time immemorial if he concluded that it was going to end. Man doesn't do that.

It is only recently with the advent of that which is called the onslaught of [the] War of Religion on this plane that man concluded an end—they must have an end in order for everyone to have their rewards. And the greatest reward of all would be the ending of this place, this [so called] terrible, awful place. And when it is finished, everyone will have their pearly gates and all the like, so everyone

wants it to end and to get [it] over with so they
can have, greedily, something they don't even
understand; all they know is they want it. So, in
order for that which is termed prophesy to be
fulfilled, an ending had to take place. Well,
everyone got their doom from that which is
called religion for it created doom. That is a
truth.

These Terrible Things Shall Not Happen

Now everyone expects for all these terrible
things to happen—they shall not happen. They
never will. The quaking is like the zipper in
your pants, aye. Your fault lines are like a
zipper on this plane, they ease to let pressure
off of the outer shelves. Your volcanoes are
steam valves of a sort that let pressure off.
This is happening in the outer shelves from the
inner core. But if a great quake happened,
nothing ever goes under for where would it go?
It only shifts and moves and squeaks for this
earth was built to give, it has to in order to
sustain its orbit. But it will not be
destroyed—it never will be, Entity.

This place was built by Gods, collective ones.
Every beautiful thing is continuously refining
itself finer and finer. The New Age will continue
on and be graceful without ever ending itself or
losing itself. That is simply the way it is. This
plane will stand and it will live. That is how it
is.

If Everyone Would Start Seeing Beauty Here

Indeed sages and seers and all the like, they are
most dishonorable entities. If everyone would
start seeing beauty here and life forever, they

would find that everyone wouldn't live in such a hurry as if there is no tomorrow. They would find that everyone would slow down and live a lot longer. It's time you started loving this beauteous place and not expecting it to end. That is how it is.

I'm Really, Really Scared About It

RAMTHA Master, I am very pleased that you have been patient.

MASTER I have a very, very great fear that things are getting out of hand politically. I have a tremendous fear that we're really going to get into a situation with our so-called enemies. The more contact people that I deal with and interview, I'm more and more convinced that it seems to be out of our hands, even though I have had the opportunity to place some people in the limelight that can voice their views. I don't know what else to do and I feel unempowered, I feel useless, I feel that I can't have any effect. I'm really, really scared about nuclear holocaust. I'm really, really, scared about it.

RAMTHA Master, it will never occur—*ever!* That which has been set into motion is called intercedence. 'Tis the same intercedence that did not permit that which is termed a country called Spain to invade a country called England. It is the same intervention that did not allow that which is termed the totality of rulership of the Persian government to rule the whole known world. It is the same interception that did not allow that which is termed the Atlatians and their wondrous intellect to destroy the world. It will *never* occur.

I tell you, there is a great and wondrous intimidation that is in the processes of occurring here that has nothing to do with that which is termed any known power here on your plane. It is a power that is coming from that which is termed beyond the North Star. It is a power more awesome than anything that has thus been created by man and his intent to defend and to destroy. The intimidation is, Master, that they will set aloft like eagles and be most visible for all of your world to see. And they can sting like scorpions and part the sea and cleave a mountain in two without any effort.

And they, Entity, are going to bring a great trembling on your earth. And the trembling will be, Master, that no one here has anything greater than the threat that lies above them. It has been appropriately called intimidation, for the whole of your world will gather like frightful ants on the seas of something coming from an unknown to plague that which is termed their nests. And yet their stings can be wholly unaffected.

Only Then Will Man Lay Down His Toys And Join Together

This is being done, Entity. That is in the process of being done because only when mankind sees there is something more venomous, more powerful, more obvious than what they have, will he lay down his toys and join together to find a way to solve the mystery that has plagued and invaded his map of war. That is purposeful. You will see it before this your decade is over with. And *you* will see it.

All that man [has] designed to annihilate the other, [the annihilation] will never occur—*never*. It is not man's [will] to destroy genealogical processes and physiological processes. [It is not man's will] to destroy [not only] their embodiment but the whole of this supportive, wondrous earth that houses a whole greater civilization within its core. It is not [man's] priority to do. Thus the interception, as it were indeed, is a wondrous, calculated ploy to intimidate man who has become arrogant to defend something that does not belong to him. And that, Master, is a wondrous day and it is upon your land.

Now, words you say, Ramtha, but who can justify that they are real? I will tell you, Master, if you are totally without means to defend yourself, I would never cast aside anything that is offered that is as arrogant and as powerful as I have just offered, for you have no other choice, you see.

Mankind is beloved God. But mankind cannot come to understand what God is until he understands himself, until he becomes so great he must humble himself of that greatness. And this intimidation is intended precisely for that. Your world will never be destroyed, Master—*never!* That which will determine the end of the earth 'tis not within the will of man to have.

One Day You Will Marvel At What Has Come To Pass

And for what is called the New Age? My beloved entity that sits here before me, you will marvel one day in that which is termed your memoirs, for all that I have told you will come to pass and you will live to see blatantly God. The whole of your world *will* change, in spite of your obvious happiness to make it even more so. So be it.

So who is going to listen to one such as I that had very poor political, diplomatic and educational credentials? Very soon everyone. Because what I have spoken has come to pass thus far and will continue for the *love* of what you are, and everyone that is so gathered here and not gathered here. That is how it is. So be it. May I give you a little advice, Entity?

MASTER Please.

RAMTHA Do not squander away your moments from happiness and the goodness of your prosperous life to live in terror of something that is wholly conjecturous. Do not live in terror when you could be spending that which is termed the brilliant tapestry of your life in hours of joy. In all the moments that you have together with your beloved woman and that which is termed the seed of your seed, live them in hours of joy and contemplation. Live this Moment of Our, called Life, to its greatest possibilities. Then you will wholly have lived. There is no thing worth not living that way. So be it.

The Hour Is Late

RAMTHA The hour is late, aye? The flowers are still blooming. For you who have come back from our audience only in the splendid past of your yesterday, you are wonderful reminders of its existence. You have learned a great deal this day in your time. Profound wisdom everyone should listen to, for through wisdom you can gain the experience through the feeling within your soul without ever being a participant. Wisdom, listened to intently, advances the entity. So all that are here have been advanced greatly this day.

What be you advanced unto? Those who grovel that their questions haven't been answered, have. You are advancing to a wiser, freer, happier entity that will become the masters of his society and of the gloom that lies heavily on the land because of the prophecies of man. But you will become the splendid fire that is within you simply by adhering to wisdom, allowing it to be.

The Right Of Mankind To Express A Truth Through The Explicit God That He Is

Of all my beloved brotheren—for that is certainly what be you—you are grand unto my being, all of you. For you who have marched for great years in a past that is long ago are here again for the advancement of a totality and the right of mankind to express a truth through the explicit God that he is. There is no religion, nor government, political figure, king, man, woman, child on this plane that has the total answer for all humanity unless they have been all humanity and have arisen above it.

Harken unto the wisdom that you hear. Harken unto the love that you feel within your being and embellish it, that the light of your being singularly, one by one, will begin to lift the ceiling of consciousness here to allow the Kingdom of Heaven to emerge which is coming forth, not from the heavens beyond, beyond, but from the depth within, within. That is where it lies. The consciousness, through this wisdom, through your acts of learning, will be added to and will be given to every living creature on the land. And soon life will become a precious thing and *every* Thing of life will be deserving of it. And all things that breathe and contemplate and exist and move and *are* shall be cherished and embellished for the God-fire that allows them to be that.

War, destruction, and perilous situations shall become nonexistent on this plane only for the remarkable discovery of a God that lies within, within the latent beings that inhabit it. It is through wisdom and *profound* love that that comes forth in the becoming of each entity, sovereign as they are. Who is lost? None. Who is forgotten? None. For even the least think you that you are adds to the virtue of consciousness by your own secret, contemplative thought.

You are known from the highest of all accord for that accord runs through your veins. You are loved individually. In this world to come, government shall be an atrocity, for it considers law to govern a mass and takes away their virtue of individualized Self. That will no longer be. The Kingdom of Heaven is God unifying and come forth from the splendid light creature from the ocean of thought that once began this remarkable journey. None here have the answers; none that teach it here on this plane have the answer. The answer is not an answer—it is a movement of profound feeling that causes change. None teaches that here.

I And That Which Stands With Me

Of you, you are all exalted, you are all beauteous, you are all cherished. I and that which stands with me have begun that which is termed a great protection upon this your wondrous plane, and shall begin to deflect that which is termed the terrible prophecies that are lying latent and waiting to be fulfilled; that life can go on for the *glory* of God which is within to become without. All of you are important in that.

You can never enslave a God. You can take away his knowledge and keep him in ignorance, but total enslavement does not exist. You are not slaves and servants and puppets and caricatures of some other divine plan that watches in harmony at your misery. You have created that yourself. And through the sovereignness of your being you are going to reverse it. All of you here will live to see the great light in the sky, in twelve days. And all of you here will live to see a magnificent kingdom emerge and civilizations come forth that you have not the slightest vision existed.

A New Wind Will Blow And Behold All That Man Dreams In His Soul

And a new wind will blow, and behold, all that man dreams in his Soul comes to pass. And God, the Eternal Isness, can get on with His Sublime Design called Life in a co-existence that is within the right of divinity; and that will be Self sought in each of you. Wisdom? Blessed is he who listens; blessed is he for he shall not have to endure another's misery to gain the benefit of it. He has gained it by listening. For all who have heard, "Blessed be you," your days in your spring will be exalted. And this year of yours shall be the great gate that will open into the marvelous future for all of you.

I am pleased with you who have gathered here this day in this wondrous place—you keep balance here. Go and live in peace, in love, in a tranquil happy spirit. Let nothing take that from you—*nothing*. It is not worth it. Live to be as free as the wind, that is when you ascend; that is when you can become all things.

My word, my Isness, my power goes through you, for you, with you, always. And ever you, contemplating your solitary being, when seemingly none look upon you, contemplate me. I shall be with you earnestly. So be it.

This audience is indeed finished. Go and be in peace.

STEPPING OFF
INTO THE
BACKDROP OF
FOREVER

L A N D   H O !

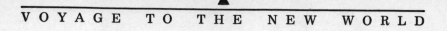

*I choose to come back in this
fashion, in this embodiment as a
woman, not to demonstrate that
a man and a woman can live
together peacefully—they can—
but [to demonstrate] that God is
both man and woman, equally
and evenly. [I choose to come
back in this fashion] to not leave
you any images that you could
dolt around your neck, or put up
on your wall, or carve into stone,
because you have always been
notorious for worshiping others.*

We Are Pleased To Have Had You Aboard

We are pleased to have had you aboard on this voyage of
exploration. To some of you this may have been your
wildest adventure ever. You may wish to throw your seat
belt aside and wait a good long spell before your next
journey. And some of you will throw your seat belt aside,
grab onto whatever you can hold on to and ride with the
wind. Why is an exploration into the unseen world so wild,
so turbulent to many of us? How can a few words,
organized in sentences, developed and punctuated into
paragraphs, and then assembled onto papyrus called a
book, cause so much excitement, so much controversy, so
much enlightenment? Perhaps because of the truths that it
delivers boldly:

What are the rules of the game, this game of
lives? Apparently, you make your own rules, you
are your own law-giver. And who is your
Savior—*You!*

What about the saying, *You can't take it with you?* According to Ramtha, you *do* take it with you, all of the treasures of your emotions gained through each life experience. All is stored within your Soul to be carried forward to your next life, your next existence, in whichever dimension you select.

If we do *take it with us,* what, then, are the punishments of failure, what are the rewards of success? Quite possibly whatever you wish them to be, for man does have that power of creation. Well, then, what is Heaven? According to Ramtha, Heaven is *all* things—Heaven is the exceedingly beautiful life that all things are for allowing us the uniqueness of our being to be. If that is so, what is hell? According to Ramtha, nothing but a shallow grave, a dump! Apparently, Man's imagination has created the awesome fear of a hell, for man does have that power of creation.

If there is no hell, what is the devil? Ramtha found him to be a masterful ploy to put the fear of God into the Souls of the little ones.

Try this thought on for size: In this age of armament, what was and is the greatest weapon ever forged? Ramtha states, "The greatest sword that was ever created was never forged of that which is termed metals; it was forged of superstition and fear. That conquered the world and still does. What a folly."

Time? According to Ramtha, time is an illusion—we can't even see an hour yet we are enslaved to this unseen illusion. There are no yesterdays, there are no tomorrows; there is only this *now-moment* to be loved with the big smile. And age? You only grow older because you think you must because you insist upon celebrating birthdays, which are really *death* days. Health? Super-health, God-health is an attitude called agelessness. And what about living in these times with a light heart? Laughter, it is the medicine of the age—to be forced into giggles is a wonder for the constitution. Laugh at least an hour a day.

And what of love? Love is the glue that holds the molecules of eternity together. And thought? Thought is the essence of God from which we all, the co-creators, create from. Genius? Genius is nothing but a receivership from the River of Thought; a receivership that brings forth new information, untold information, to the planet.

The Sun? Ramtha states the Sun is a ball of thought congregated into a mass that feeds us all—every moment we are bathed in the Light of God. Brotherhood? We are all brothers, we are all sisters, emanating from the same Source, the Father Principle, Who judges us not, Who only *loves* us.

And of relationships? All for the fun of it, all for the experiences that are imparted upon the Soul, that will become wisdom that won't have to be experienced again. And for what purpose is life? To discover the beauty of you—the awesomeness of your power, the compassion of your humility, the childlikeness of your love.

The truths which this book embraces are delivered to you under the major subject heading, *New Information For Humankind*. The information will provide many with cocktail conversation and many with dream material. The information is presented in total freedom for only one purpose—because you are loved. The information presented in this navigational aid will help to begin the release of the bonds that have enslaved humankind for literally thousands of years. This information brings forth points of view which are rarely discussed in these times. And from where does this information emanate? This information has been brought forth via an entity who exists in a world that we have not the eyes to see.

Could worlds exist that we can't see? In the days of Columbus nothing existed beyond the shores of Spain. It was an explorer who brought forth the wonders of the unseen world in those days, the North American continent. And even today do we see all that there is around us? Ironically, all of us are sustained by that which we can't see—oxygen.

Many of us today are forming beliefs that, indeed, an unseen world *could* exist. We have formed these beliefs because we have been touched by the unseen world, not in an evil way but in a loving way. And that *touch* has brought new understandings of ourselves and new interrelationships with others. That touch has brought forth a new happiness that doesn't depend upon outside influences but is forever inside. And now many of us are seeing new perspectives of the Universe in which we live.

I suppose it could be said that many of us have been anxious to receive this new information, so it has come forth to breathe a sigh of relief to our Souls, who knew it all along. The answers are simple, yet complex. And every answer seems to have its other side which complicates and then completes its circle. For what purpose is existence? To exist. For what purpose is creation? To create. For what purpose is life? To live. Every moment, you walk in the Presence of God. Every moment, you look upon the Presence of God. Every moment, you hear the Song of Creation. Yet, we do not live these truths in our seen realities. We do not *know* they are so. In our moments of doubt, our unseen friends emerge to state conclusively, *It is so.*

Each and every one of us is a reflection of our own Self. When we truly *love* our Self, we will love all others. When we despise the others, we despise a bit of us. When we curse at an *other,* we curse our Self. According to Ramtha, "Self love is where world love begins." Simple concepts, yet the complexities abound.

We live in absolute abundance, yet each month, for many, bills remain unpaid. The abundance that we live in is within us. When we become sovereign over the pence we can have all we want; we will have then tapped into the Source. There are those who have turned the search for abundance into *a fun dance.* There are others who haven't unlocked their doors to the Source, who still live in the limitedness of lessness, lackings.

And what of the gent who continuously manifests, yet he manifests in the negative? Even the negative has its purpose for good for it is a step to success. And, if it works in the negative, it will work in the positive.

What is the difference between patience and waiting? Patience is representative of a God who *knows* he is aligned to the Universe and is cognizant as the Universe adjusts to his will and the will of others. *Waiting* is impatienceness.

What will we become? The answer is, what we *are.* To many, this answer will seem ludicrous. To many, this answer is ultimate. To the intellectual who clamors for explanation, proof, those proofs are apparently on their way. To the feeler, the *beamer,* they simply know. How do they know? It simply *feels* right. According to Ramtha, feelings are the ultimate reflection of Godness.

And what do all of these feelings and understandings lead us to? A place of total contentment, total Isness, and *total* knowingness. A place without rules and regulations because those who live there accept and know their God-responsibility. A place of absolute freedom and total abundance that floats in the purity of love. And what does all of this feel like? A total release into unlimitedness without a re-lease to another limitedness; a flight without wings; a movement without purpose; a love without pain; a moment without the ache in the gut.

This voyage that you've just completed asks nothing of you, yet it asks everything of you. It is a reminder, reminding you of that which you are. It is a puzzle, a mind-puzzler that may even force you into some decisions that might bring some *fire* into your life. And for some who rest in "success," that fire might be called excitement, for success in these times is certainly synonymous with boredom.

And perhaps a few soulmates will find each other; perhaps a few will turn that soulache into their soulmate while finding a new happiness along the road to Self. Or you may decide to shift your career. And there will be some rough seas ahead, if you call them forth. And there will be smooth sailing ahead, if you set your heading accordingly. Destiny is a series of moments tied together by the thread of feelings. Destiny is remade every instant, every moment, as you live the truth that you are.

A God-Maker Extraordinaire

Ramtha is a God-maker. He is calling forth immaculate, impeccable, humble entities who know the power that they

be and who live in absolute evenness in perfect alignment
with God, the Father, the Source.

> *What grand temple has been erected for God's
> greatness, his esteemed principle, his awesome
> beauty? Can any place capture the morning rods
> of a golden sun? Or the beams of the enchantress
> when she is in full bloom at midnight as her
> children, the stars, twinkle and dance in the
> heavens? There is no place that has ever been
> made that could honor such an entity that is all
> things, except in you.*

Who is this God, the Father, the Source, that Ramtha
continually speaks of? Ramtha is presenting for your
consideration a totally new and unlimited definition of the
essence of God. Instead of finding a God that is judgmental and vengeful, a God to be feared, Ramtha has found
a God who is to be loved, a God that is judgeless, who
overflows with unconditional love for the all of creation.
What supports Ramtha's statements of the existence of a
non-judgmental God? Ramtha's reasoning has its astounding simplicity: If God is everything, if He were to judge
anything, He would be judging Himself.

So, then, who is responsible for the tomorrows of your
dreams? Destiny is remade every instant, every moment,
as you live the truth that you are. Therefore, in every
moment, *you* are remaking your destiny. And you make
that destiny according to how you feel about it. If you *feel*
the God that you are, every moment will be an unlimited
moment in the presence of God. If you *feel* the limitedness
of what you see, your moments will be bound to that limitedness. *You* are ultimately responsible for your tomorrows.

To expand yourself into horizons unlimited, see beyond
sight into forever. Know that your processes are *your*
processes, *your* workings, and *your* becomingness. And

know that your processes are ongoing, infinite, immortal. Is there any proof to immortalness? You be the judge.

Why Have I Returned In This Form?

RAMTHA There are many entities that have passed from this plane, that have done many grand things, that have gone many places. I am the only one that ever came back. For, you see, I have been a man, I have lived in desperate situations, I have been all that you have been. The justifiableness of me returning in this form was that all that you have been I have mastered and thus ascended unto my kingdom.

I choose to come back in this fashion, in this embodiment as a woman, not to demonstrate that a man and a woman can live together peacefully—they can—but [to demonstrate] that God is both man and woman, equally and evenly. [I choose to come back in this fashion] to not leave you any images that you could dolt around your neck or put up on your wall or carve into stone, because you have always been notorious for worshiping others.

If there was no image to remember with me—other than that I have loved you and I have tolerated you, and you I—what you would remember of our union is *how you feel* and that, alas, is the most important thing of all. When you leave I, 'tis not that you remember me but that you remember *you* and the God that I have, over and over, through great repetition, expressed to you and demonstrated to you is there—rich in flesh and color and blood and vibrance and blue and brown and all colors—It is there.

But of this form, that the purpose and the reason that I was here is to tell you how *important* that you are. Because the only way that one enters into the Kingdom of Heaven, 'tis not through the worship of another but the worship of the All. And the only way you can ever comprehend the All is from *your* point of view. And *your* point of view is called God and that is where you find Him. How do you think, my beloved people, that you ever become? By following someone else, by worshiping something you never saw and never understood? You become by worshiping *you.*

This Illusion Was Purposely Played Upon You

This illusion, as you would have it that way, was purposely played upon you to deny [you] the accessibility into Ramtha, the identity, so that all you [would] have to worship is *you.* That is when you see God, that is when you live in joy, that is when you know all things—when it is through *you.* I am exceedingly pleased and fervent within my being that this *outrageous* entity hath pulled it off, and even more so be you when you find out just how grand that you are.

I leave you with this little, what you would call, advice—I call it knowingness. Take what you have learned, what your have heard, what you have read, and apply it with simplicity. The simpler you become the more powerful you will become. And if you want something, *ask* for it. No one on this plane is in power to give it to you—they play games with you and if you are wanting games you will have them. If you *want* something, ask from the Lord God of Your Being that the Father give it to you and He will, regardless of what it is. And where do you go? You need not that which is termed a gilded temple. You need only to go [to] a quiet place and ask, it is heard.

Do Remember What I Have Taught You

Remember what I have taught you—The Father and You are One; The Kingdom of Heaven is within You; What you want life to be, desire it and then *live* it, it is there for the taking. Put them into practice. And when we come together again, I will take you a step further and closer to where I am. So *be* it.

[A toast]

To *Life!*

You have listened very well;
you have forgotten your questions.
It was a good audience.

Ramtha, The Enlightened One

▲

Sources

Ramtha Dialogue Tapes

February 7, 1981, Ojai, California
February 13, 1981, Calabassas, California
April 25, 1981, Calabassas, California
November 22, 1981, Boston, Massachusetts
February 6, 1982, Calabassas, California
February 7, 1982, Calabassas, California
March 21, 1982, Seattle, Washington
January 9, 1983, Calabassas, California

Books

The World Aloft by Guy Murchie,
Bantam Books/Houghton Mifflin, 1983 Edition